CAMBRIDGE LIBRARY COLLECTION

Books of enduring scholarly value

Religion

For centuries, scripture and theology were the focus of prodigious amounts of scholarship and publishing, dominated in the English-speaking world by the work of Protestant Christians. Enlightenment philosophy and science, anthropology, ethnology and the colonial experience all brought new perspectives, lively debates and heated controversies to the study of religion and its role in the world, many of which continue to this day. This series explores the editing and interpretation of religious texts, the history of religious ideas and institutions, and not least the encounter between religion and science.

Forty-One Facsimiles of Dated Christian Arabic Manuscripts

The twin sisters Agnes Lewis (1843–1926) and Margaret Gibson (1843–1920) were pioneering biblical scholars who became experts in a number of ancient languages. Travelling widely in the Middle East, they made several significant discoveries, including one of the earliest manuscripts of the Four Gospels in Syriac, a dialect of Aramaic, the language probably spoken by Jesus himself. Their chief discoveries were made in the Monastery of St. Catherine on Mount Sinai. This fascicule, originally published in 1907 as part of the Studia Sinaitica series, is a collection of Arabic Christian documents from various sources, including St. Catherine's Monastery and the British Museum. Translated and edited by Lewis and Gibson, the texts, of great value to scholars of Arabic Christianity, include portions of theological treatises, sections of the Gospels and tales from the lives of the saints; of particular interest are the pages of biblical commentary and lectionaries.

Cambridge University Press has long been a pioneer in the reissuing of out-of-print titles from its own backlist, producing digital reprints of books that are still sought after by scholars and students but could not be reprinted economically using traditional technology. The Cambridge Library Collection extends this activity to a wider range of books which are still of importance to researchers and professionals, either for the source material they contain, or as landmarks in the history of their academic discipline.

Drawing from the world-renowned collections in the Cambridge University Library and other partner libraries, and guided by the advice of experts in each subject area, Cambridge University Press is using state-of-the-art scanning machines in its own Printing House to capture the content of each book selected for inclusion. The files are processed to give a consistently clear, crisp image, and the books finished to the high quality standard for which the Press is recognised around the world. The latest print-on-demand technology ensures that the books will remain available indefinitely, and that orders for single or multiple copies can quickly be supplied.

The Cambridge Library Collection brings back to life books of enduring scholarly value (including out-of-copyright works originally issued by other publishers) across a wide range of disciplines in the humanities and social sciences and in science and technology.

Forty-One Facsimiles of Dated Christian Arabic Manuscripts

EDITED AND TRANSLATED BY
AGNES SMITH LEWIS
AND MARGARET DUNLOP GIBSON

CAMBRIDGE
UNIVERSITY PRESS

CAMBRIDGE UNIVERSITY PRESS

Cambridge, New York, Melbourne, Madrid, Cape Town,
Singapore, São Paolo, Delhi, Mexico City

Published in the United States of America by Cambridge University Press, New York

www.cambridge.org
Information on this title: www.cambridge.org/9781108043526

© in this compilation Cambridge University Press 2012

This edition first published 1907
This digitally printed version 2012

ISBN 978-1-108-04352-6 Paperback

FORTY-ONE FACSIMILES
OF DATED CHRISTIAN ARABIC
MANUSCRIPTS

CAMBRIDGE UNIVERSITY PRESS WAREHOUSE,
C. F. CLAY, Manager.
London: FETTER LANE, E.C.
Glasgow: 50, WELLINGTON STREET.

Leipzig: F. A. BROCKHAUS.
New York: G. P. PUTNAM'S SONS.
Bombay and Calcutta: MACMILLAN & CO., Ltd.

Frontispiece.

Sinai Syriac and Arabic Palimpsest of Peshiṭta Gospels.
f. 86 a.
Script. inf.   John xix. 34 b—40.
Script. sup.   Homily of Mar Jacob.

STUDIA SINAITICA No. XII

FORTY-ONE FACSIMILES
OF DATED CHRISTIAN ARABIC
MANUSCRIPTS

WITH TEXT AND ENGLISH TRANSLATION

BY

AGNES SMITH LEWIS,

HON. D.D. (HEIDELBERG); LL.D. (ST ANDREWS); PH.D. (HALLE)

AND

MARGARET DUNLOP GIBSON,

HON. D.D. (HEIDELBERG); LL.D. (ST ANDREWS)

WITH INTRODUCTORY OBSERVATIONS ON
ARABIC CALLIGRAPHY

BY

THE REV. DAVID S. MARGOLIOUTH, LITT.D.

LAUDIAN PROFESSOR OF ARABIC IN THE UNIVERSITY OF OXFORD

CAMBRIDGE:
AT THE UNIVERSITY PRESS

1907

𝕮𝖆𝖒𝖇𝖗𝖎𝖉𝖌𝖊:

PRINTED BY JOHN CLAY, M.A.

AT THE UNIVERSITY PRESS.

TO THE

VICE-CHANCELLOR

AND SENATUS ACADEMICUS

OF THE ANCIENT UNIVERSITY

OF ST ANDREWS

THESE SPECIMENS OF DATED

CHRISTIAN ARABIC MSS

ARE RESPECTFULLY DEDICATED

BY

AGNES SMITH LEWIS

AND

MARGARET DUNLOP GIBSON

AS A TOKEN OF GRATITUDE

FOR THE HONOUR CONFERRED ON THEM

ON APRIL 2ND, 1901

PREFACE.

THE present volume is a natural sequel to Mrs Gibson's Catalogue of the Arabic MSS. in the Convent of St Catherine on Mount Sinai, which forms the third number of this series. The idea of compiling it was first suggested to us by the late Dr Robertson Smith, who remarked, "Arabic dated Manuscripts are just what we want." But it was only in 1897, on the occasion of our fourth visit to the Convent, that we set about photographing specimen pages in earnest, choosing, so far as possible, pages which tell their own tale about chronology. The dates have been re-verified by Mrs Gibson at Sinai both in 1902 and in 1906. They are sometimes misleading, as a date which at first appeared trustworthy has been found on closer examination to belong, not to the MS. in which it appears, but to that from which the said MS. was copied; or again it may merely be the record of a special examination of the MS. by some important person several centuries after it came into being. Therefore if in any case there should be a discrepancy between a date given in this volume and one already published in No. III. *Studia Sinaitica*, the former is always to be preferred.

We have tried to give at least one specimen of each century, between the eighth and the eighteenth inclusive. For our illustration of the eighth century papyrus we are indebted to the kindness of Dr B. Moritz, Director of the Khedivial Library, Cairo, who allowed us to photograph it. Strictly speaking, this is not a Christian document, but neither is it a specially Mohammedan one. By Mr A. G. Ellis of the British Museum, we were guided to Nos. II. III. XXVIII. XXX. XXXII. all of which were photographed by Mr Donald Macbeth, while M. Léon Dorez of the Bibliothèque Nationale, Paris, did us a like service with regard to No. XXVI. We owe special thanks to Dr Bernard Grenfell, of Queen's College, Oxford, for deciphering the few crabbed lines of Greek commercial cursive on the papyrus. They are not now difficult to read, with the help of his copy; but before that copy was made, they had baffled us as much as driftwood from the Atlantic Ocean baffled the

Spaniards before the discovery of America. We have also to thank Professor Edward Granville Browne, of Cambridge, for a few hints about the Arabic words on that papyrus. Professor D. S. Margoliouth, of Oxford, has helped us in the understanding of some obscure phraseology, especially in Nos. V. IX. XIV. XVI. XXXI. XXXV. XXXVII. and XXXVIII. and has also kindly executed a task which exceeded our competence, and which was yet necessary for the utility of the book; we mean the Introductory Essay on its calligraphy.

In conclusion, as we are told by Deacon Simeon, the copyist of No. XXXVI. that imperfection exists in the soul of Nature, and the defects of the sons of Nature are not unknown; we would echo his prayer that every one who reads in this book, and finds any defect or fault and puts it right, God may put him right in this world and in the other one.

AGNES SMITH LEWIS.

MARGARET DUNLOP GIBSON.

INTRODUCTORY OBSERVATIONS.

THE study of Christian Arabic, which had scarcely commenced when Dozy published his Supplement to the Arabic Dictionaries in 1881, has now become fairly popular. Besides a variety of Christian Arabic texts published in England, France, and elsewhere, we have now a sketch of the history of Christian Arabic literature and an account of its dialect, both from the pen of Dr G. Graf. The present publication richly illustrates its palaeography.

The chief predecessor of Mrs Lewis and Mrs Gibson in this field is the very eminent Arabist H. L. Fleischer, in the third volume of whose *Kleinere Schriften* are republished three papers (from the *Z. D. M. G.* for 1847, 1861 and 1864) accompanied by plates, illustrating Christian Arabic scripts. Facsimiles of several are also to be found in the beautiful volume edited for the Palaeographical Society by the skilful hand of the late Dr W. Wright. Some specimens of the Christian Arabic MSS. of the Sinai Library were published in facsimile in the Cairene Journal *Muktataf* for 1894 (XVIII. 367): they were taken from a large number put into the hands of the editors, the nature of whose magazine prevented their using the whole. Some photographs of MSS. from the same collection are given by Mrs Gibson in Nos. II. and III. of *Studia Sinaitica*, and in Nos. VII. and VIII. of the same series; also by Mrs Lewis in *Horae Semiticae*, No. III. In the Russian publication called *Zapiski Vostochnavo Otdyelenia* XVI. (1905) there are three plates from the Sinaitic MS. 460.

The subject has not ordinarily been treated independently, owing to the difficulty of separating Christian from other Arabic writing. Perhaps the name "Christian type" may be assigned to the handwriting illustrated in the frontispiece, in *Studia Sinaitica*, III. p. 89, and XI. Plates 1—8, and in the Russian publication quoted : perhaps too facsimiles II. and III. show a tendency to introduce Syriac forms into Arabic letters, or at least give the latter a suggestion of the Syriac script. And in general, if the Christian documents of the fifth century A.H. and later be compared with contemporary Moslem documents, a certain stiffness, a certain approximation to the "square character" is often found in the former which is not found in the latter. The Moslem scribe seems to work with greater ease and greater certainty. The Moslem leaves something to the reader, the Christian allows no ambiguity for him to settle.

Nevertheless the main tendencies in the development of Moslem calligraphy were reproduced in the Christian scripts, for reasons which can
easily be made out. Zealous Moslems of an early period forbade non-
Moslems to acquire the Arabic language: in the charter given to the
Christians by Omar it is expressly stipulated that the former shall not read
or write Arabic or use the Arabic language (von Kremer, *Kulturgeschichte*,
I. 102, 3). This rule was presently found so vexatious to both conquerors and
conquered that it had to be relaxed. And when the Arabic language came
to be used in the bureaux, Christians and members of other tolerated sects
were known to be specially qualified for clerical work. The *Kātib Naṣrānī*,
"Christian Secretary," is a person who meets us constantly in Moslem
history: and though many a ruler issued edicts forbidding the employment
of non-Moslems in any government posts, the force of circumstances caused
these edicts to be speedily annulled. A record of their enforcement and
repealing meets us most frequently in the history of the Mamluke dynasty,
but examples occur far earlier: Omar II. (100 A.H.) issued an edict of this
sort (Von Kremer, *ibid.* II. 167), and in 501 A.H. (Ibn al-Athīr, Cairo 1303,
X. 160) a vizier resumes office on condition that he employs no non-
Moslems. The Christian or other non-Moslem secretary was frequently
compelled to personate a Moslem in his official compositions, and even
to exhibit familiar acquaintance with the Coran. Thus the famous
Secretary of State Ibrāhīm Ibn Hilāl, who was a Sabian, "associated with
Moslems on the friendliest terms, fasted with them during Ramaḍān, and
knew the Coran so well by heart that it floated on the tip of his tongue
and the nib of his pen" (*Letters of Ibrāhīm*, Lebanon, 1898, p. 5). There
were indeed pious grammarians who would sooner starve than teach an
Unbeliever the Coran, or even the grammar of Sibawaihi, in which verses
of the Sacred Book were to be found: but the ordinary teacher could not
afford to be particular. And it would seem that the chief teachers of writing
as well as the great grammarians were ordinarily, if not always, Moslems.

The writing of the Christians was from this cause assimilated to that of
the Moslems: and to write well was a step on the road to promotion.
"There was (says Ṭabarī, III. 1181) a certain Fadl Ibn Marwān, attached
to a provincial governor, as writer: and he wrote a good hand. Presently
he was associated with a clerk of Muʿtaṣim (afterwards Caliph), and wrote
under his supervision: on this man's death Faḍl got his place, and himself
had a clerk under him. His fortunes rose with the fortunes of Muʿtaṣim,
he went with him to Egypt, and got control of the whole wealth of the
country. Before Maʾmūn's death he came to Baghdad, and acted for
Muʿtaṣim, giving such orders as he thought fit in Muʿtaṣim's name: when

Mu'taṣim came to the capital as Caliph, Faḍl was the real Caliph, having under him all the bureaux." Similar stories of promotion starting with the possession of a good handwriting are common : and the fortunate persons were often Christians and sometimes Jews.

On the other hand Arabic never became the religious language of any Christian sect, or of the Arabic-speaking Christians as a whole : whence the ordinary cause for the development of a special script was wanting. Syriac, Coptic, or Armenian, remained the religious language of the Christian communities, even (in the first two cases) after the majority of the people had ceased to understand them. Syrians, Jews, and Samaritans, when writing Arabic for purposes connected with the religious communities to which they belonged, often preferred to employ their national alphabets. When they used the Moslem script, it was ordinarily to their interest to conceal rather than to flaunt the fact that they did not belong to the Moslem community.

A considerable number of books written by Christians were of course intended for the public market. Such were medical and philosophical treatises and in general works dealing with science. In these the religion of the author appears in the nature of the formulae with which his book opens and closes : otherwise there may be little or nothing whereby it can be detected. But even translations of the Old and New Testaments were often intended for all classes of readers. And the better sort of Mohammedan theologians and historians, such as Ibn Ḳutaibah and Fakhr ad-dīn ar-Rāzī, exhibit a fair acquaintance with their contents. On the whole then in the case of works written in both the language and the script of the Moslems, it is best to suppose that the authors usually intended contributing to the national literature of an Arabic-speaking country, rather than to that of their own religious community only. We are therefore prepared to find the modifications of the script noticeable in works emanating from the leading community imitated by those of subordinate communities. The facsimiles therefore should be studied side by side with other works illustrating the development of Arabic handwriting, such as those appended to the Oxford and Berlin Catalogues of Arabic MSS., the *Aegyptische Urkunden aus dem königlichen Museum zu Berlin*, and Moritz's magnificent *Arabic Palaeography*. For the origin of the Arabic script we cannot do better than refer to Berger's *Histoire de l'Écriture dans l'Antiquité* (Paris, 1891). A list of works by Arabic writers on the theory and practice of calligraphy is given by Ahlwardt at the beginning of vol. I. of his monumental *Arabic Catalogue*. Examples of different styles of hands are given by A. P. Pihan, *Notice sur les divers genres d'écriture ancienne et moderne des Arabes*, etc. (Paris, 1856). The treatise called *Khaṭṭ u Khaṭṭāṭān* of

Habib Efendī (Constantinople, 1306 A.H.) contains little besides biographical notices of leading calligraphers.

Facsimiles I. II. III. stand apart from the rest, as representing decidedly early forms of writing. A well-known tradition ascribes the invention of diacritic points to the instigation of the famous or notorious proconsul al-Ḥajjāj Ibn Yūsuf. "Abu Aḥmad al-ʿAskarī in his work on textual corruption states that people continued reading out of the Coran of ʿUthmān Ibn ʿAffān for over forty years to the days of ʿAbd al-Malik Ibn Marwān: by that time the amount of textual corruption had become very serious and spread over the whole of ʿIrāḳ, so that Ḥajjāj had recourse to his scribes and asked them to invent diacritic signs for the letters that looked alike: and it is said that Naṣr Ibn ʿĀṣim undertook this task. He invented the dots, single and in pairs with differences of position. For a long time people continued to write all their texts with dots. Even so however corruption of the text was found to occur, and they invented the system which is called *iʿjām*, which they employed in addition to the dots" (Ibn Khallikān, I. 155). The date of Ḥajjāj[1] (on whom M. Périer has recently published an exhaustive study) is the first century of Islam—he died in 95: the first of the Lewis-Gibson facsimiles is of a deed written eight years before that event, 87 A.H. The dots being still novelties, we are not surprised to find no trace of them in the deed. Karabaček, on the basis of an exhaustive study of papyri, finds evidence for the employment of the diacritic dot under B in documents dated 81—96 and for that of the double dot under Y in documents dated 82—89 (*Denkschr. der Wiener Akademie, ph.-hist. Kl.* XXXIV. 225).

Facsimiles II. and III. are similar to the handwritings described by Fleischer in the papers referred to above. Of the first we might use his description, "ein steifes, sich noch eng an das Kūfī anschliessendes Neskhī." The wide space left after the non-attached letters is similar to that in Fleischer's Tab. V. On the other hand, except for the sign of the feminine the points seem regularly employed, and indeed in the Eastern style, and the vowel U is occasionally inserted. The writing however of the two dots over the sign of the feminine is a proceeding which some grammarians at least do not recognize: thus in the *Maḳāmah* of Ḥarīrī (No. VI.) which contains an epistle with alternate words of dotted and undotted letters, the sign of the feminine is treated as undotted.

An archaism common to these two hands is the protraction of the stroke

---

[1] An example of the difficulty occasioned by the want of dots in Ḥajjāj's time is given in Mubarrad's *Kāmil*, I. 291, ult. (Cairo, 1308.) Jāḥiẓ, *Ḥayawān*, i. 55, implies that in the time of Hishām Ibn ʿAbd al-Malik (ob. 125 A.H.) a dotted letter could not be confused with an undotted one.

of the Alif below the line of the letter to which it is attached. The Jīm and two following letters resemble in their angle a Syriac G: the Dāl is of the form of a Nestorian D; the Ṣād is almost rectangular: the Ḳāf (medial) resembles an Estrangelo Q: the final Kāf is similar to Dāl and to Ṭā; the medial Mīm is above, not below the line; and the medial form of the Hā resembles the initial. Finally in facsimile III. there are specimens of the Kufic final Nūn, and final Yā, and also of a Syriac ʻAin. Probably in facsimile III. the writer's hand is decidedly influenced by the habit of writing Syriac.

The writing of the frontispiece is curious, and exhibits many archaisms, especially in the forms of the Dāl and Ṭā: the hook at the top of this letter and at the top of the Lām is also found in the MS. of which there is a facsimile in the *Muḳtaṭaf* XVIII. 367 (fig. 3) as well as in facsimile III.

Archaic handwritings are usually preserved (1) in sacred books, (2) on coins, (3) in inscriptions. In these sorts of writing the old style was long maintained by the Moslems. Since the Arabic versions of the Bible had only a moderate degree of sanctity attaching to them, it was natural that the Christians should extend to their religious books, as well as to others, the modifications that became popular in the writing of the national language. Yet deliberate attempts at reproducing the script of an old copy are not wanting. Ibn Khaldūn notices that men often intentionally imitated the bad writing of a saint, hoping to be spiritually benefited thereby.

On the history of Arabic writing there is a passage of some length in the Bibliography of Ḥājji Khalīfah (III. 149), the bulk of which is taken from the *Fihrist* (pp. 7—9). Since neither of these authorities give illustrations, their statements are very hard either to understand or to criticize. The author of the *Fihrist* (377 A.H., 987 A.D.) mentions Ibn Muḳlah (ob. 328 A.H.) as the finest penman (with one other) of all who had lived up to his time: but he does not make the assertion which we find in later writers (e.g. Ibn Khallikān, II. 81) that Ibn Muḳlah was the person who altered the Arabic script from the Kufic to "the present style." This change is sometimes however assigned to a later penman, Ibn al-Bawwāb (ob. 413 or 423, Ibn Khallikān, I. 436), whose calligraphy was so famous in his own time that even a *blind* poet (Abu'l-ʻAlā of Maʻarrah, *Siḳṭ al-zand*, II. 44) could draw an image from it. Of course the supposition that either of these writers invented *naskhī* is contradicted by the fact that the *naskhī* type goes back to the very commencement of Arabic writing. Still it is likely that the influence of these calligraphers was very great, and it is noticeable that the change from the type of facsimile III. to that of facsimile IV. is much the most decided in the collection; the first of which is before, the latter after Ibn Muklah's time. The manipulation of the script is altogether more facile, somewhat like that of a grown-up person as compared with the rigidity and stiffness of a child's handwriting. In facsimile IV. we see the first examples (in this collection) of the practice of distinguishing the *un*dotted letters by writing minute forms of them underneath (in the case of Ḥa, Sīn, Ṣād, ʿAin) or a sign above (chiefly in the case of R and Sīn). Perhaps the distinction of the undotted letters in this way is what is meant in the passage quoted from al-ʿAskarī by *iʿjām*, since its purpose was to provide extra security against corruption, after the dots had been found insufficient.

The methods employed are collected by Wright in his *Arabic Grammar*, I. 4, to whose observations one is added by Salhani in the Preface to *al-Akhṭal*, p. 7. The volume of Ḳalḳashandī which he quotes has not yet been issued by the authorities of the Khedivial library. Most varieties will be found illustrated in the facsimiles, but it is not yet possible to assign their employment to special ages or schools. The *muhmilah* sign (as these are called) over the Sīn of the word Masīḥ (Christ) in facsimiles XXI. XXV. and XXXIII. seems intentionally to take the form of a cross. The sign on the Sīn of Yasūʿ (Jesus) is in the form of an acute angle, with the apex downwards. On other words in the same page (facsimile XXI.) it takes the form of a line slightly inclined from the horizontal, originally meant for a repetition of the letter itself. In facsimile XXII. this is used for the Sīn of Yasūʿ. In facsimile XII. it is a curved line, still more suggestive of the original letter. In facsimile XXXIII. it takes a form very similar to that of the hamzah, except in the case of Masīḥ, where the cross is retained. The hamzah form is again found in facsimile XXXVII. The letter which most frequently takes a *muhmilah* sign in these facsimiles is the Rā: the Dāl is scarcely ever, if at all, thus distinguished. There are however quite late MSS. in which the scribe regularly puts a dot under it[1].

The epoch marked by the work of Ibn Muklah is equally apparent in the facsimiles published by Wright: compare his Plate XX. of 272 A.H. with Plate XCVI. of 348.

The alterations which handwriting underwent in Eastern Islam after this time were slight. According to Ibn Khaldūn (translated by de Slane, II. 399) another epoch was marked by the copies of Yāḳūt of Mausul (ob. 618 A.H.) and the Saint ʿAlī al-ʿAjamī: Ibn Khallikān (ob. 671) knows

---

[1] An example is the Bodleian MS. of Yāfiʿī's History.

of Yākūt as a calligrapher, but does not, like Ibn Khaldūn, state that his writing formed the model followed throughout Eastern Islam. Ḥajjī Khalīfah adds some more names: the geographer Yākūt (ob. 628) and Yākūt al-Mustaʿṣimi (ob. 698), "whose fame filled the earth." Probably then the type of writing in use in the seventh century (A.H.) was set by Yākūt of Mausul, the type in use in the eighth by Yākūt al-Mustaʿṣimi. Ḥajjī Khalīfah adds that the styles of writing in which these persons excelled were six: Thulth, Naskh, Taʿlīḳ, Raiḥān, Muḥaḳḳaḳ, Riḳāʿ. Several of these are mentioned in the *Arabian Nights* (ed. Macnaghten, I. 94, cited by Dozy). Ḥabīb Efendī observes that the *Raiḥānī* style suits Corans and Prayers, the *Naskhī* Commentaries and Traditions, the *Thulth* Histories, the *Tauḳiʿ* Firmans and Rescripts, the *Riḳā* Letters, the *Muḥaḳḳaḳ* Verses. He adds that in *Thulth* four parts are straight, and two round; in *Muḥaḳḳaḳ* 1½ parts straight, and the rest round; in *Tauḳiʿ* they are equally divided. Plate XI. of our facsimiles belongs to the Riḳāʿ style: in letters (says Ḥajjī Khalīfah) it is undesirable to insert dots, except where there is some danger of ambiguity: to insert them all is rather to imply that your correspondent is unskilled in reading hands. The writer of this MS. (though it is not an epistle) is decidedly sparing with them. He also has a tendency to omit the "teeth" of the Sīn, and to attach the non-connecting letters to those that follow (e.g. in maḳṣūd, line 9). All these are found in facsimile V. (of the fourth century), and even in very early specimens of Arabic writing (see Abel, no. 6 of the year 259 A.H., 873 A.D. as read by Karabaček, *W. Z. K. M.* XI. 12). The others are all naskhī, though X. and XXVI. show a faint tendency towards taʿlīḳ.

It now becomes the problem of the palaeographer to discover clues by which to date undated MSS.: and this problem is no easy one, although numbers of facsimiles of the same century put together (as they are here and in the Moritz collection) leave a distinct impression of uniformity on the mind; it is however hazardous to attempt to fix the date at which any particular form of letter first came into use, or that at which it went out of fashion. Indeed such innovations as can be traced seem ordinarily to be the introduction into the Naskhī hand of forms already in use in the Riḳāʿ hand.

The perpendicular form of the connected Dāl and the final Nūn resembling Rā which occur in facsimile IV. seem characteristic of that period (later fourth century A.H.). At this period too the (final or isolated) Bā and Tā are often unfinished towards the left; facsimile VI. (which is much later, 551 A.H.) illustrates this practice better than IV. Experts in handwriting will very probably be able to observe much more.

The persistence of the employment of the initial for the final Kāf is very noticeable. The final form (similar to final Lām, only that the latter is below the line) meets us first in facsimile XIX. (671 A.H.), line 2: in facsimile XXIII. a similar form, with a top stroke, is found in line 1, whereas the employment of the initial for the final form occurs in the same page. In XXI. the initial form is used (684 A.H.), and examples of it occur as late as 994 (facsimile XXXIV.). The form with a minute kāf inserted (looking like a hamzah) is found in facsimile XXVI. (714 A.H.). With this handwriting generally compare Ahlwardt XX. of 804 A.H. The employment of both the minute kāf and the top stroke (which most calligraphers regard as an inelegance) is found in facsimile XXXVI. (1036 A.H.).

The forms of the Alif retain some archaisms in quite late MSS.: so the protraction of the connected form below the line is illustrated in XV. (A.H. 619), but perhaps not later. The form (isolated) in which the bottom curves towards the left appears in quite recent MSS. (e.g. facsimile XXXI., A.H. 994). A form in which the top is hooked towards the left occurs chiefly in the inelegant writing of facsimile XIV. (A.H. 600).

Among the principles of calligraphy analysed by Ḥājjī Khalīfah after Abu'l-Khair one is that attention should be paid to what is called "justifying," i.e. seeing that the lines begin and end at the same point. Some of the facsimiles (e.g. VII. XVIII.) show clear signs of the line or lines employed for the guidance of the scribe in this matter. The treble dots at the commencement of many of the lines in facsimile XIII. probably serve the purpose of the inverted comma, a sign similar to which is often found in Western MSS.: if this be the purpose of the dots, the places for them have not always been felicitously selected. The use of the Hā to fill up a line that would otherwise be imperfect, which occurs in facsimile XV., is common in Arabic MSS.

The Mohammedan custom of prolonging the B of *Bism* in the Invocation at the commencement of books or chapters was, as Fleischer observed, imitated by Christians: facsimiles XIV. and XXIX. offer good examples. The prolonged B is said to be compensation for the loss of the Alif in this formula.

The orthography and vocalization belong to the subjects of which Dr Graf has treated rather than to palaeography. Both are frequently faulty.

D. S. MARGOLIOUTH.

INTRODUCTORY NOTES.

THE manuscript which has supplied us with a frontispiece is not dated. It was discovered by Mrs Gibson in 1902 and is therefore not included in the Syriac and Arabic catalogues which we made in 1893. Our reason for placing it in this volume springs from a wish to make its existence better known. It is numbered 514, and is noted in Mrs Gibson's Catalogue of the Arabic MSS. in the Convent of St Catherine on Mount Sinai (*Studia Sinaitica* III.) as an ἀφηρημένον. The story of how she found it is in the *Expository Times* for 1902, pp. 509, 510.

The manuscript is a palimpsest. It has a stout binding much broken at the back. The leaves are of good, fine vellum, measuring about 23 centimètres by 15.

The upper script is Arabic, in a hand which has been assigned to the end of the IXth or beginning of the Xth century, and is considered to be an exclusively Christian one. A specimen of the same writing is to be seen in Plate XX. of the Palaeographical Society's facsimiles, Oriental Series. It is from the Vatican Codex Arab. 71 which is dated A.D. 885; and another specimen is in the upper script of a palimpsest belonging to me, and of which I have published several facsimiles in No. XI. of this series.

The text of the upper script in Sin. Arab. 514 contains four sermons by Jacob of Serug. The first one, with which the book in its present defective condition begins, is on the subject that no man may alter the least value of anything which our Lord has said in the holy Gospel.

The remainder of the text is for the most part a martyrology. The names of the martyrs are not very easy to identify; but Mrs Gibson observed those of Philemon, Euthalius, Cyricus and Julitta, Eustratius and Arsenius.

Mrs Gibson says: "I could decipher little of the under script without using the reagent (hydrosulphuret of ammonia), but, whenever I painted a page with it, the Syriac lines came up clearly, and were very easy to read. I consider this handwriting to be not later than the VIth century, but I am not an expert, and it seems to me probable that, being a palimpsest, it may be the oldest Peshitta in existence. Its appearance tells at once that it is not quite so ancient as the Old Syriac palimpsest discovered by Mrs Lewis in 1892. I had ample opportunity to place the two together, and there can be no question about their relative antiquity.

"The first page I tried was f. 162^b which began at John vii. 10, col. 1, ending at ἄλλοι in *v.* 12. Col. b began at *v.* 16 and ended at *v.* 18. This shows that the leaves of the original Syriac manuscript have been folded in two to meet the wants of the Arabic martyrologists in the IXth or Xth century."

On f. 173^b Mrs Gibson found part of the *Transitus Mariae* in Syriac, but she does not believe there is much of it.

In the binding is a fragment of a Syriac hymn in honour of the Virgin.

Our second facsimile is from a photograph taken by Mr Macbeth. The slightly Cufic form of some of the letters speaks for its antiquity. It is the earliest dated Arabic MS. in the British Museum. Its author, Theodore Abu Ḳurrah, Bishop of Harran and Nisibis, lived about the end of the IXth century, and was a pupil of St John of Damascus. It contains a treatise on Image worship which has been published by Dr J. Arendzen, and also, in its first part, a Defence of Christian Doctrines, of which a portion has been edited by P. L. Malouf, S.J., in the *Machrig* (Vol. VI., No. 22, p. 1011). Dr Malouf adduces reasons for believing that the treatise which occupies the first part of the volume is due to the same Theodore Abu Ḳurrah. He also states his conviction that Or. 4950 is the oldest dated Christian MS. extant.

This MS. has furnished the subject for a paper read by Professor Burkitt before the Cambridge Philological Society in 1896 on St Charitan. He maintained that the rare Syriac words ܣܩܐ and ܣܩܘܬܐ and the Arabic word سيق are equivalent to the Greek word Λαύρα, which originally meant "alley" or "lane." Mrs Gibson, before she had heard of this paper, identified the word سيق with the Greek σηκός which means "a fold." We both think that the Arabs are much more ready to assimilate (and often to mangle)[1] a foreign word than to translate it. My friend Dr Porphyrius Logothetes, the present learned Archbishop of Mount Sinai, tells me that this term was in ancient times applied to what is now called the Βῆμα, that is the space screened off from the body of the church just behind the holy table. That the Βῆμα should have been used as a *scriptorium* will surprise no one who has become acquainted with the habits of Oriental priests. But the origin of سيق may possibly be more humble and modern. Archbishop Porphyrius has suggested that it probably comes from a habit which the Greeks have of calling a church, and also a monastery, ὁ οἶκος. They say, for example, that they are going εἰς οἶκον, "to a church, or to a monastery," and the Arabs may easily have shortened it into سيق by dropping the first and last syllables, just as they have turned εἰς τὴν πόλιν into Stamboul or Istambûl. English scholars will please remember that the Greeks pronounce οἶκον "eekon." As the word is again used in No. XXXV. with the sense of "cloister" it was evidently also applied to the whole monastery, which might well be called a fold.

[1] Cf. Gawâlîkî, *Almu‘ Arrab* (Sachau), p. 5: اعلم انهم (العرب) كثيرا ما يجترئون على تغيير الاسماء الاعجمية اذا استعملوها.

We have not been able to find the text of No. XIV. in any printed book. There was more than one Evagrius or Evaristus connected with Constantinople, from the Bishop who reigned in A.D. 370 to the celebrated historian who accompanied Bishop Gregorius of Antioch to that city in the VIth century. The emperor to whom this apology is addressed appears to be Constantinus VII. Porphyrogenitus. It belongs therefore to the close of the VIIIth century.

The Greek text of No. XVI. will be found in the works of Gregory Nazianzen, Oratio XXXII., cap. IX. This is numbered XXI. in the Sinai MS.

The Syriac text of No. XX. is in the Roman edition of Mar Ephraim, vol. I., p. 172. It is the beginning of the Sermo in Patres Defunctos.

In the last line of No. XXII. we at first found وهو له وللامرة . برسم قلايته untranslateable and were inclined to adopt the suggestions of the Sheyk Muhammed 'Asal to read وللامة and تلايته, translating "it belonged to him and to the community in the order of its reading." But Professor Margoliouth thinks that امرة is the plural of the Syriac word ܐܡܘܪܐ or ܐܡܘܪܐ, cantor (see *Thes.*, p. 245).

We have failed to find the text of No. XXVI. in any of Mar Ephraim's works.

The extract from the Lives of Saints which appears in No. XXVIII. is practically the same as what I have already published in the Mythological Acts of the Apostles, page 83 (*Horae Semiticae* III.).

A text which nearly corresponds to that of No. XXXII. will be found in the Arabic version of Joseph ben Gorion, printed at Beirut in 1872.

The Greek text corresponding to No. XXXVIII. will be found in *Migne's Patrologia*, vol. LXIII., pp. 16, 17.

The Greek and Latin text of XXXIX. will be found in Migne, vol. LXXXVIII., pp. 627, 628, and that of XL. in the same volume, pp. 1207, 1208.

All the MSS. which have furnished us with specimen pages are paper, with the exceptions of Nos. II., III. and the frontispiece, which are vellum, and No. I., which is papyrus.

But this does not raise the suspicion as to their antiquity which would occur to us in the case of codices written in Europe. Paper was used in the East for several centuries before it was known to the Westerns. It had not made its way to the neighbourhood of Antioch in the year when John of Beth Mari, the Stylite, turned a manuscript of the Old Syriac Separate Gospels into one of the oldest of extant palimpsests by writing his biographies of Holy Women above them, but we find the story of its origin clearly told in Dr Karabaçek's Introduction to his "Guide to the Museum of the Archduke Rainer Papyri." Two Chinese papermakers were taken prisoners by the Arabs in a battle where the latter defeated the combined forces of the Chinese and the Turks at Kangli, on the banks of a river named Tharâg in Transoxonia, in July A.D. 751, accounts of the battle being extant in the chronicles of both victors and vanquished. These papermakers continued to practise their craft in Samarkand, and about A.D. 790 a Government paper-factory was established at Baghdad during the reign of Harûn al Raschid. The Chinese made thin paper of the bark of the mulberry tree; and the Arabs produced a more serviceable article out of linen rags. Flourishing factories for its manufacture existed in Arabia, Egypt, Syria, and North Africa long before it found its way into Europe by way of Damascus, under the name of *charta Damascena* or *charta bombycina* from the town of Hierapolis, which was then called Mambidsah of Bombyca. It is therefore not surprising that our third facsimile, although it is taken from a paper manuscript, bears the date of A.D. 988 although there are no extant Greek paper manuscripts before the middle of the XIIIth century[1].

There are 47 dated Arabic manuscripts in the library of St Catherine on Mount Sinai. Fifteen of these are not included in this volume. In two cases we have given a second example from the same manuscript, because the date page did not offer a good specimen of the hand-writing.

[1] Cf. *Encyclopaedia Britannica, sub* "Paper."

AGNES SMITH LEWIS.

DESCRIPTION OF MANUSCRIPTS.

II. British Museum, Or. 4950, vellum, 237 leaves, most of them $7\frac{3}{4}$ inches by $6\frac{1}{4}$. The lower outward corner of each leaf is invariably rounded off.

III. British Museum, Or. 5008, vellum, 53 leaves, $8\frac{1}{4}$ inches by 6.

IV. Sinai 139, paper, about 167 leaves, 21 × 14 centimetres.

V. Sinai 580, paper, about 206 leaves, 20 × 16, from 8 to 12 lines on page.

VI. Sinai, paper, about 195 leaves, 18 × 13.

VII. Sinai 69, vellum, about 147 leaves, 18 × 13.

VIII. Sinai 417, vellum, about 303 leaves, 21 × 17.

IX. Sinai 410, paper, about 165 leaves, 17 × 12.

X. Sinai 97, paper, about 383 leaves, 5 being blank, 14 × 10.

XI. Sinai 445, paper, about 435 leaves, 16 × 11.

XII. Sinai 82, paper, about 241 leaves, 22 × 13.

XIII. Sinai 117, paper, about 139 leaves, 23 × 16.

XIV. Sinai 420, paper, about 193 leaves, 29 × 22.

XV. Sinai 13, paper, about 383 leaves, 25 × 16.

XVI. Sinai 276, paper, about 355 leaves, 24 × 16.

XVII. Sinai 122, paper, about 221 leaves, 25 × 17.

XVIII. Sinai 408, paper, about 161 leaves, 36 × 25.

XIX. Sinai 95, paper, about 329 leaves, 18 × 14.

XX. Sinai 439, paper, about 359 leaves, 22 × 14.

XXI. Sinai 104, paper, about 269 leaves, 3 being blank, 21 × 14.

XXII. Sinai 89, paper, about 194 leaves, 28 × 21.

XXIII. ⎫
XXIV. ⎭ Sinai 99, paper, about 209 leaves, 30 × 22.

XXV. Sinai 91, paper, about 249 leaves, 22 × 14.

XXVI. Bibliothèque Nationale, Paris, Fonds Arabe 159, paper, 170 leaves, $25\frac{1}{2}$ centimetres by 17, 15 lines on each page. Dated in the year 1130 of the Martyrs.

XXVII.   Sinai Cod. Arab. 397, paper, about 267 leaves, 31 × 21.

XXVIII.   British Museum, Or. 1327, No. 8 in Supplementary Catalogue, paper, dated 1050 Anno Martyrum. Paper, 242 leaves, 9½ inches by 6¾. Evidently written in Egypt. The sections are marked in the margin by the hand of the scribe with Coptic numerals.

XXIX.   Sinai 628, paper, 23 × 17.

XXX.   British Museum, Or. 1330, No. 14 in Supplementary Catalogue, paper, dated Wednesday the 1st of Mesuri, Anno Martyrum 1102. Paper, 267 leaves, 10 inches by 6½. The author is Ephrem Syrus, but his name is not given.

XXXI.   Sinai 398, paper, about 304 leaves, 36 × 20.

XXXII.   British Museum, Or. 1336, No. 31 in Supplementary Catalogue, paper, 169 leaves, 9 inches by 6¼. The date A.H. 899 is given from the earliest of several notes recording that the MS. had been read by someone. It is therefore probably older than A.D. 1493, though apparently of the fifteenth century.

XXXIII.   Sinai 121, paper, about 360 leaves, 28 × 20.

XXXIV.   Sinai 135, paper, about 208 leaves, 28 × 21.

XXXV.   Sinai 264, paper, about 208 leaves, 24 × 16.

XXXVI.   Sinai 423, paper, about 615 leaves, 36 × 21.

XXXVII.   Sinai 625, paper, about 108 leaves, 20 × 15.

XXXVIII.   Sinai 626, paper, about 230 leaves, 31 × 22.

XXXIX. ⎫
XL.   ⎬ Sinai 339, paper, about 179 leaves, 21 × 15.

XLI.   Sinai 587, paper, about 23 leaves, 14 × 18.

I.

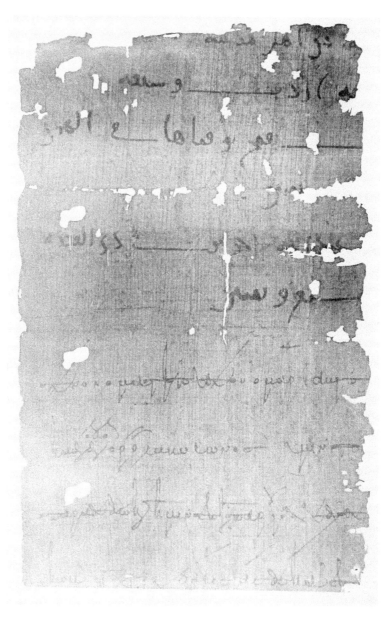

Papyrus.
Khedivial Museum, Cairo.
Eighth Century.

ERRATA

Page xx, l. 6, *for* Mambidsah of Bombyca *read* Mambidsch or Bambyce.

Page 1, l. 7, *for* o μαρ ϛ αβιπ ... *read* Ομαρ غ αβιπ ...

„ l. 13, *for* † 6172 *read* † 617⅔.

Page 3, last line, *for* Epistoler *read* Cantor.

Page 43, l. 4, *for* الانجيلين *read* الانجيليين ; l. 16, *for* نيرين *read* النيرين, delete note 4.

Page 44, l. 13, *for* "the continuance of the lights, his rule," *read* "as long as the sun and moon endure."

Page 81, l. 25, *for* حركسندوس *read* خريسندوس.

Page 82, note, *for* ἐλείσον *read* ἐλέησον, and delete [1] after Chrysandus.

I. KHEDIVIAL MUSEUM, CAIRO. PAPYRUS.
EIGHTH CENTURY.

كل اهل مدينَه . . . . . .

اردب وسبعة ع[شر]

قمح توفياها فى الهدن ─────

. . . . .

عبد الله اخر يوم فى ذى القعدة

سَبع وثمنين*───

θ

εν ονοματι του θεου ο μαρ ϛ αβιπ . . .

καθολ(ικῶν) ὁρρ(ίων) βαβυλωνος υμιν το(ῖς

παραδεδωκ(α)τ(ε) ημιν επι τ(ης) παρού(σης) ἰνδ(ικτι)ο(νος) εδ( ) θε(

κωμ(ης) ἀρτ(αβας) χι3β′† εξακοσια . δεκα επτ(ὰ δίμοιρον

* A.H. 87 = A.D. 705.   † 6172

وجمع السليس ثلاثون واحد وسبعون ٠ اما
اسقف ا و قسيس ا و شمامس لو اعنك لمو
اسلط لايصوم ار بعين يوما الصيام العام
و الجمعه و الاربعا فليقطع الاان يعذرابعد
جسد يمنعه من ذلك وار كان علماان يقرد
نو المصحف بعون الله وقوته و نعمته
و كان كمال كتابه ه اول يوم من فسير
يكون من حساب سني الدنيا علما بقل ه
كنيسه القيامه بيت المقدس سنه مبنه الا ش
وللثمانيه وشعه وستو و من سني الاكسندر سنه
الف ومايه و ثمنيه و ثمنين و يكون من سني اليون
ه سهو ربيع الاول من سنه اربع وستو و ماتس
كتبه الفاي المسكين الحقير اصطاى
بن حكم بعو د بالاولى سوى طاري يكو
لمعلمه الاب الفاضل الطهر ابو وجاى اناسس
عمه الله ه بادانت هذا ت فا ذكر ه لا
تسا لا تسك الله و اقامك عن يمينه و اسعد
ذلك النصوص التي المصوب المعوج اد يقول
تعالوا يامبار كي اي دنوا الملك المعد لكم من قبل
انشا العالم يكون لنا ذلك شفا عه مرتر يم الطاهره
ومار يعنا و صلوات جميع الابا الابرار امين و امين

Treatise on Christian Theology
probably by Theodorus Abu Kurrah, Bishop of Harran.
British Museum Oriental MSS. 4950.
f. 197 b.
A.D. 876.

II. BRITISH MUSEUM ORIENTAL MSS. 4950. A.D. 876.

*Treatise on Christian Theology probably by Theodorus Abu Kurrah,
Bishop of Harran.*

f. 197ᵇ ∴ ايما ∴ قانون واحد وسبعين : لمجمع السليحين ∴
اسقـف او قسيس او شمـاس او اغنسـط او
ابسلط لا يصوم اربـعـيـن بـوما الصيام العام
والجمعة والاربعـا فليقطع الا ان يـعـتـل بمرض
جسد يمنعه من ذلك وان كان علمانى يفرز ⊙
تـمز المـصـحف بعون اللـه وقوتـه ونعـمـتـه
وكان كمال كتابته¹ فى اول يوم من ذقمبرس
يكون من حساب سنى الدنيا على ما يقبل فى
كـنيسة القيامة بـيـت المقدس سنـة ست الاف
وثلثمـاية وتسعة وستين ومن سنى الاكسندرس سنة
الف وماية وثمنية وثمنين ∴ ويكون من سنى العرب
فى شهر ربيع الاوّل من سنة اربع وستين ومايتين
∴ كـتـبـه الخاطى المسكـين الحقـير اصطافـنى
بن حكم يعرف بالرملى فى سيق مارى حريطن
لمعلمه الاب الفاضل الطهر الروحانى انبـا بسيل
عـمـره اللـه ⊙ اذا انت قـرات فـاذكـرنى لا
تنسا لا نسيك اللـه واقامك عـن يمينه واسمعك
ذلك الصوت البـهى المحبـوب المُفرح اذ يقول
تعالوا يا مباركى ابى رثوا المُلك المُعد لكم من قبل
انشا العالم يكون لنا ذلك بشفاعة مرتمريم الطاهرة
ومارى يحنا وصلوات جميع الابا الابرار امين وامين
∴   ∴   ∴

¹ Cod. كتابه

To the Council of the Apostles. The seventy first Canon. Whosoever
is Bishop or Elder or Deacon or Reader or Epistoler, let him not fast

forty days of the general fasts ; and on Friday and Wednesday let him abstain (from flesh) unless he be excused through bodily illness which prevents him from this, and if he be a layman, let him separate himself. The Book is finished, by the help and power and grace of God ; and the completion of its writing is on the first day of December, according to the reckoning of the years of the world which is accepted in the Church of the Resurrection of the Holy House (Jerusalem), in the year 6369; and of the years of Alexander the year 1188 ; that is, of the year of the Arabs in the first month Rebi' of the year 264. It was written by the poor contemptible mean Stephen son of Hakm known as the native of Ramleh in the cloister[1] of Mar Haretin, for his Teacher, the noble and pure and spiritual father, Anba Basil ; God give him long life ! When thou readest, remember me, forget not, may God not forget thee ! and may He place thee at His right hand, and cause thee to hear that beautiful and beloved and gladdening voice when He shall say 'Come, ye blessed of my Father, inherit the kingdom prepared for you from before the foundation of the world.' May this be ours through the mediation of the pure Lady Mary and of Mar John, and the prayers of all the righteous Fathers, Amen and Amen.

[1] Gr. σηκός

Apostolical Constitutions and Canons of Councils.
British Museum OR. 5008.
f. 53 a.
A.D. 917.

III. BRITISH MUSEUM OR. 5008. A.D. 917.

Apostolical Constitutions and Canons of Councils.

f. 53ª السمك واخر عشار · فان قيل لك هذا فقول من شا منكم فليقيم
لنا ميت واحد ولا ينال ان يكون حراث او دباغ · والا فاصغر من هذا
يضع يده على مريض فليبرا منه ايضًا انما عمل الاسقف . واخذ لتنقية
الانفس بالفعال والكلام يرفعها بالحركات الفاضلة الى الله
ويكون وديع شريف العقل مثل مراة بهية مقرب عن رعيته القرابين
النقية حتى يصيرهم قربان نقى لله . فاما غير ذلك فنجبه عنى
اغريغوريوس المتكلم فى اللاهوت¹ اياكم اعنى يا اصحاب المراتب
فكونوا عين ليس مملوة ظلمة لكيما لا نكون قواد الى الشر
لان النور اذا كان هكذا فالظلمة ماذا تكون منه ايضا ليس يعطا
الله عطية افضل من النية · فانت لا تقدم ابدا شى شبهها فاعطى
ما يعطا المساكين فان كرا الزانية لا يقسم نقى تقى ان اراد يعطى
قليل طيب افضل ممن يعطى كثير غير نقى منه ايضا اعلم ان
الجمال هو العقل ليس الذى تبيه الايادى او يحله الزمان فان نظرت
الى ما تنظر فاعلم ان السماحة سماحة العقل
تم والسبح والمجد والعظمة والوقار للاب والابن وروح
القدس من الان وكل اوان والى دهر الداهرين امين وكتب
الخاطى دانيال بن ارسين فى شهر نيسان من سنة خمس وثلثماية
فكل من قرا او سمع يترحم على من كتب رحم من كتب ومن قرا ومن لملا امين

¹ Cod. الاهوت

fisherman, and another a taxgatherer. And if this be said unto thee,
say: Whosoever of you will, let him raise up one dead man to us, and
it does not matter if he be a husbandman or a tanner, and if not, then
something less than this, let him lay his hand on a sick person, and let
him be also healed by him; for it is the work of a bishop, and he is

appointed for the purification of souls in deeds and words; that he may raise them by excellent movements towards God. And let him be gentle, noble in understanding, like a clear mirror, bringing pure offerings from his flock that he may form them into a pure offering unto God. But yet besides this let us answer him, as saith Gregorius the Theologian, O ye! I mean O men in authority! be ye an eye not filled with darkness, so that ye may not be guides into wickedness; for when light is thus, what will result from darkness? God has given no gift more excellent than conscience. And as for thee, thou never offerest anything like it. And give what He giveth to the poor. For the wages of a harlot are not distributed purely and reverently. And if he wishes to give, a little good is better than if one gives much that is not pure. Also know that beauty belongs to the reason, not what hands can prepare, nor time destroy. And if thou look to what thou seest, know that gifts are the gifts of reason.

It is finished. Praise and glory and might and honour be to the Father and the Son, and the Holy Ghost, henceforth, and always, and for ever and ever, Amen. And the sinner Daniel son of Arsîn wrote [this] in the month of Nisân of the year 305. And whosoever readeth or heareth, let him pray for mercy on him who wrote it. [May God] have mercy on him who wrote and on him who readeth it and on him who hath dictated it. Amen.

IV.

Lectionary of the Gospels.
Sinai Cod. Arab. 139.
f. 111 b.
A.D. 988.

IV. SINAI COD. ARAB. 139. A.D. 988.

Lectionary of the Gospels.

John 18.25   f. 111ᵇ

فقالوا لـه لعلك مـن تلاميذه انت فـكـفـر ذلك
وقـال لست انـا فقال لـه واحد مـن عبيد راس
الكـهـنة كـان نسيب للذى قـطـع بطرس اذنـه
انـا رايتك فى البستان معه فكفر ايضا بطرس
وللوقت صـاح الديك فاصعدوا يسوع مـن عـنـد
قـيافا الـى البلاط وكان بكرة وهم لـم يدخلوا
البلاط ليلا يتنجسوا من اجل انهم يريدوا ياكلون الفصح ∴

Matt. 26.57

تقرا يوم الجمعة الكبيرة بالليل انجيل ثالث من متى
فى ذلك الزمـان امسكو الشرط ليـسوع وجـآوا١
بـه الى قيافا راس الكـهـنة حيث اجتمعوا الكـهـنة
والمشيـخة فامـا بطرس فلحقه من بعيد حـتى بلغ
دار راس الكـهـنة فدخـل داخـلا وجلس مـع
الـخـدام لينظـر اخر الامـر · ثـم ان راس الكـهـنة
والمـشيـخـة كـلـهـم كـانوا يطلبون شـهادات

¹ Cod. وجاو

And they said unto him, Perhaps thou art one of his disciples? And he denied it, and said, I am not. And one of the servants of the High Priest said unto him, being a kinsman of the one whose ear Peter had cut off, I saw thee in the garden with him. And Peter denied again. And immediately the cock crew. And they made Jesus go up from beside Caiaphas to the palace, and it was morning, and they went not into the palace, lest they should be defiled, because they wished to eat the Passover.

To be read on the Great Friday, in the evening. The third Gospel, from Matthew. At this time the officers took Jesus, and went with him to Caiaphas the High Priest, where were assembled the priests and the elders. But Peter followed him afar off, till he arrived at the palace of the High Priest. And he went in, and sat with the servants, to see the end of the matter. Then the High Priest and all the Elders sought for witnesses.

V.

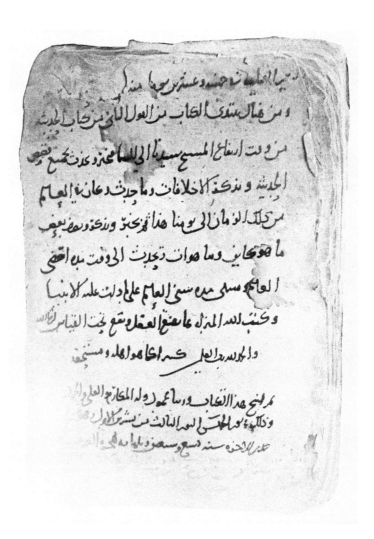

Legends and Histories.
Sinai Cod. Arab. 580.
f. 206 b.
A.D. 989.

V. SINAI COD. ARAB. 580. A.D. 989.

Legends and Histories.

. . . . ريس العملية فى خمسة وعشرين يوما منذ

ومن هناك نبتدى الكتاب من القول الثانى من كتاب الحديثة

من وقت ارتفاع المسيح سيدنا الى السما فنخبر ونحدث بجميع قصص

الحديثة ونذكر الاختلافات وما حدث وكان فى العالم

من ذلك الزمان الى يومنا هذا ثم نخبر ونذكر ونصف بعض

ما هو كاين وما هو ات ويحدث الى وقت مدة انقضى

العالم ومنتهى مدة سنى العالم على ما دلت عليه الانبيا

وكتب الله المنزلة بما يقنع العقل ويقع تحت القياس . ان شاء الله

والحمد لله رب العالمين كثيرا بما هو اهله ومستحقه

تم نسخ هذا الكتاب وربنا عمود وله المكارم والعلى والجود

وذلك فى يوم الخميس اليوم الثالث من تشرين الاول وهو سنح

جمدى الاخرة سنة تسع وسبعين وثلثمایة لهجرة العرب

master of mechanical arts in five and twenty days since...and from thence
we begin the book with the second discourse of the book of the New
Dispensation, from the time of the Ascension of the Christ our Lord to
Heaven and we will tell and relate all the stories of the New Dispensation;
and we will record various things, and what happened and existed in the
world from that time till this our own day; then we will tell and record
and describe something of what exists and of what is to come, and what
will happen until the time when the world shall come to an end; and
the end will be the period of the years of the world according to what

the prophets shewed about it, and the books of God which have come down, according to what satisfies the intellect, and comes under analogy, if God will. And much praise be to God the Lord of the worlds, to which He has a claim and a right.

The copy of this book is finished, and our Lord is a stay, and His are the virtues and the nobility and the generosity. And this was on Thursday the third day of the first Tashrin (November); and this is (the last day of) Jumādā II., in the year 379 from the Arab *Hegira*.

VI. SINAI COD. ARAB. 106. A.D. 1056.

Gospels.

f. 45^b Matt. 24. 46 الذى يوافى مولاه فيصادفه كذلك عاملا · 47 الحق

48 اقول لكم ليقيمنه على جميع ماله ∴ 48 هوان يزعم ذلك

49 العبد السو فى قلبه ⊙ ان سيدي يبطى فى مجيه 49 فيبدا

يضرب العبيد فى جملته ويواكل ويشارب

50 السكارى ⊙ 50 فياتى سيد ذلك العبد يوم لا يرجى ⊙

51 وساعة لا يعلم ⊙ 51 فيشقه شطرين[1] ⊙ ويجعل حظه

مع المرائين ⊙ هناك يكون البكا وصريف

الاسنان ⊙ سبت سابع عشر ⊙ وعيد الشهيدات

Matt. 25. 1 حينيذ تشبه ملكوة السما لعشرة عذارى

2 اللاتى اخذن مصابيحهن وخرجن للقا الختن خمس

3 منهن كن عاقلات وخمس جاهلات 3 فاخذن

4 الجاهلات مصابيحهن ولم ياخذن معهن زيتا 4 واما

5 العاقلات فاخذن زيتا مع مصابيحهن 5 فلما احتبس

6 الختن نعسن كلهن ورقدن 6 فحين كان نصف

الليل اذا بصوت ينادى هوذا الختن قد اتى| اخرجوا

7 للقاه 7 عند ذلك قمن العذارى كلهن واسرجن

8 مصابيحهن 8 فقلن المايقات للحليمات اعطونا

9 من زيتكن لان مصابيحنا تنطفى 9 فاجبن العاقلات

¹ Cod. سطرين

who [when] his lord cometh and findeth him, so doing. ⁴⁷Verily I say Matt. 24.46
unto you, that he will set him over all that he hath. ⁴⁸But if that evil
servant shall say in his heart, "My lord delayeth in his coming"; ⁴⁹and

shall begin to beat all the servants and to eat and to drink with the drunkards. ⁵⁰ And the lord of that servant shall come in a day when he expecteth not, and [in] an hour when he knoweth not; ⁵¹ and shall cut him in two halves, and shall appoint his portion with the hypocrites; there shall be weeping and gnashing of teeth.

The seventeenth sabbath. The feast of the women Martyrs.

Matt. 25. 1 ¹ Then shall the kingdom of heaven be likened unto ten virgins, who took their lamps, and went forth to meet the bridegroom. ² Five of them were wise, and five were foolish. ³ And the foolish took their lamps, and took no oil with them. ⁴ But the wise took oil with their lamps. ⁵ And while the bridegroom was detained, they all slumbered and slept. ⁶ And at midnight a voice called "Behold the bridegroom cometh; go ye out to meet him." ⁷ Then all those virgins rose, and trimmed their lamps. ⁸ And the stupid said unto the learned, "Give us of your oil, for our lamps are going out." ⁹ And the wise answered,

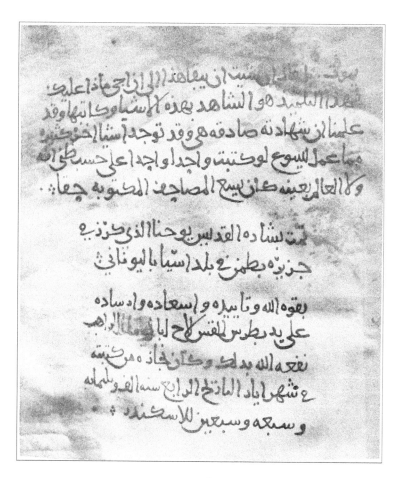

VII

Gospels.
Sinai Cod. Arab. 69.
John xxi. 23—25.
A.D. 1065.

VII. SINAI COD. ARAB. 69. A.D. 1065.

Gospels.

يموت · بل قال ان شيت ان يبقا هذا الى ان اجى ماذا عليك · John 21.23

24 فــهـــذا التلميذ هو الشاهد بهذه الاشيا وكاتبها وقـد

25 علمنا ان شهادته صادقة هى وقد توجد اشيا اخرة¹ كثيرة

مما عمل يسوع لو كتبت واحدا واحدا على حسب ظنى انه

ولا العالم بعينه كـان يسع المصاحف المكتوبة حقا ·:·

تمت بشارة القديس يوحنا الذى كرز فى

جزيرة بطمز فـى بلـد اسيا بـاليونانى ·:·

بقوة الـلـه وتـاييـده واسعـاده وارشـاده

على يد بطرس القس الاخ ابا كرميلا الراهب

نفعه الله بذلك وكان نجازه من كتبته

فى شهر ايار التاريخ الرابع سنة الف وثلثماية

وسبعة وسبعين للاسكندر ·:·

¹ Cod. اخر

die: but He said, If I will that he tarry till I come, what is that to thee? And this is the Disciple that testifieth of these things, and wrote them; and we know that his testimony is true. And there are found many other things which Jesus did, if they were written one by one, according to what I think, the world itself would not in truth contain the written books.

The Gospel of Saint John is finished, he who preached in the isle of Patmos in the country of Asia, in Greek.

By the power of God, and His strengthening and blessing and guidance, by means of Peter the Presbyter, the brother, father (Carmelus?) the monk, may God give him profit by this, and his completion of his writing was in the month of Ayar (May), the date was the fourth day (Wednesday) in the year 1377 from Alexander.

VIII.

Martyrdoms, etc.
Sinai Cod. Arab. 417.
f. 120 b.
A.D. 1095.

VIII. SINAI COD. ARAB. 417. A.D. 1095.

Lives of Saints.

f. 120^b واستفنس ⊙ هولا كانوا فى مملكة قلوذيوس ⊙

وفى امارة فيقاريوس الملقب بهولينوس

الرومولى ⊙ وكان كنصورينوس مقدما فى

اصحاب الراى رتبته ماجسطرس ⊙ فسعى به

وقرر فاعترف بالمسيح وطرحوه فى الحبس

فلما صارت فى الحبس عجايب كثيرة فى جملتها

انه انهض ميتا امن بالمسيح جميع الجند الذين

اتفقوا هناك فضربت اعناقهم ⊙ ثم احضرت

ذهيبة المغبوطة فعلقوها فى سهم عجلة وقر

زوا جنبيها بالضرب بسياط من اعصاب

البقر وطنبوها مسحاء على ظهرها فوق الارض

وضربوها بالعصى الجافية واحرقوا جنبيها

بمشاعل نار وطرحوها فى الحبس واخرجوها

منه بعد ستة ايام فطحنوا بالحجارة فكيها

وفتتوا برمانات رصاص فقار ظهرها ⊙ ثم علق[وا]

فى عنقها حجرا وزجوها فى غمق البحر وتمت

شهادتها ⊙ وصفينوس المغبوط ضربوه على ع[نقه]

برمانات ثقال وعلقوه فى خشبة ⊙ ضربوه

بسياط من اعصاب البقر واحرقوا جنبيه

وجوفه بمشاعل نار

and Stephen. These were in the reign of Claudius, and in the jurisdiction of Vicarius, surnamed Paulinus Romulius. And Kensurinus was distinguished amongst the Counsellors; his rank was that of a Magister.

And he was accused about it, and was stedfast, and confessed the Christ. And they flung him into prison. And when many miracles happened in the prison amongst his fellows—for he raised a dead man— many of the soldiers who happened to be there believed in the Christ, and their necks (heads) were struck [off]. Then the blessed Zahîbat[1] was brought out, and they bound her to the pole of a cart; and they stung her sides by scourging with whips of ox-hide; and they stretched her out naked on her back upon the ground; and they beat her with thick sticks, and burnt her sides with firebrands; and flung her into the prison. And they brought her out of it six days afterwards; and they crushed her jaws with stones; and they broke the *vertebrae* of her back with weights of lead. Then they hung a stone to her neck and threw her into the depth of the sea; and she finished her martyrdom. And the Blessed Safinus, they beat him on the neck with heavy weights, and hanged him on a piece of wood; and they scourged him with whips of ox-hide; and burnt his sides and his entrails with firebrands.

[1] $= X\rho\upsilon\sigma\hat{\eta}$.

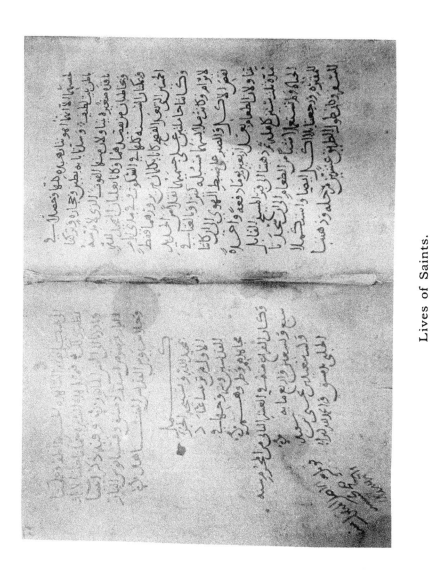

Lives of Saints.
Sinai Cod. Arab. 410.
ff. 163 b, 164 a.
A.D. 1103.

IX.

IX. SINAI COD ARAB. 410. A.D. 1103.

Lives of Saints.

مارانة وكورة

f. 163ᵇ لجنسهما لا انهما اهونتا بهذه كلها وحصلا فى
باطن بيت لطيف ∵ وسدتا بابه بطين وحجارة وتركتا
نافذة صغيرة يتناولان منها القوت الذى لا بد منه
ويخاطبان من يقصدهما وكانا يعلدان التمجيد لله .
ويمكثان السنة كلها فى السكوت وفى مدى ايام
الخمسين التى بعد الفصح كانا يكلمان من يزورهما فقط
وكانتا حاملتين على جسميهما ثقلا من الحديد
لا يرام وكانت ملابسهما مسبلة كثيرا وبالغتا فى
نقص الاكل والصبر على ضبط الهوى الى ان كانتا
يتناولان الطعام بعد اربعين يوما دفعة واحدة
مدة ثلث سنين كاملة . ثم ذهبتا الى قبر المسيح القابل
الحياة ولم تستعملا شيا من الطعام الى ان سجدتا
للمقبرة ورجعتا بلا اكل ايضا واستكملا
السفر وكان طول الطريق عشرين مرحلة وذهبتا

f. 164ᵃ الى هيكل ثقله الشاهدة الحسنة الظفر وعملتا
نظير ذلك فبمثل هذه السيرة جملتا جنس الاناث
وبادرتا الى الختن الماثور ∵ وفيه ذكر ابينا
البار قرصوم اسقف دمشق وقسيانوس البار
وجلاسيوس القديس الشاهد ∵

كــــــــــــــمل

بتمجيد الله وتسبيحه الجزء
الاول من ترتيب اعياد
القديسين وشروحها فى
مجاهدهم . وطرقهم ∵
وكان الفراغ منه فى العشر الثانى من المحرم سنة
سبع وتسعين واربع ماية
وكتب سعيد بن يحيى بن سعيد
الحلبى بدمشق والحمد لله كثيرا

قوبل الاصل المنقول منه
وصح بحسبه والحمد لله كثيرا

[they were noble] in their race; but they despised all this, and reached the interior of a pleasant house; and they closed up its door with clay and stones, and left a little window, that through it they might receive their necessary food, and converse with those who came to them, while loudly uttering praise to God. And they remained the whole year in silence, and for the space of fifty days after Easter, they talked only to those who visited them. And they carried upon their bodies an unbearable weight of iron; and their dress was very flowing; and they exceeded in reduction of food, and in patience in the regulation of desire until they partook of food once after forty days for the full space of three years; then they went to the grave of the immortal Christ; and they did not use any food until they worshipped at the sepulchre; and they returned also without food and completed the journey, and the length of the road was twenty days' journey, and they went to the temple of Thekla the martyr, the glorious in victory; and they did like this, and thus glorified the race of women, and they hastened to the chosen Bridegroom. And in it there is a remembrance of our righteous father Carsum Bishop of Damascus, and of the righteous Cassianus, and of Gelasius, the holy one, the Martyr.

Finished.

to the glory and praise of God, the first part of the order of the feasts of the saints, and its exposition of their conflict and their ways; and its completion was in the second decade of Moharram in the 497th year. It was written by Said son of John son of Said of Aleppo, at Damascus, and much praise be to God.

In another hand. Collated with the original from which this was copied, and found to be correct in accordance with it; and great praise be to God.

VI.

Gospels.
Sinai Cod. Arab. 106.
f. 45 b.
A.D. 1056.

X.

Gospels. Epistle to the Hebrews
and Sermons.
Sinai Cod. Arab. 97.
f. 2 a.
A.D. 1123.

X. SINAI COD. ARAB. 97. A.D. 1123.

Gospels, Epistle to the Hebrews and Sermons.

f. 2ª بــــــم الاب والابــن وروح الـــقــدس

الاه واحد نبدا باسم ربنا يسوع المسيح

نكتب بشارة مثاوس الانجيلى الطاهر

اول قراة منه تقرا فى ليلة الميلاد الطاهر

Matt. i. 1 المقدس سفر كــينونة يسوع المسيح

2 بن داود بن برهيم · ابرهيم ولد اسحق

اسحق ولد يعقوب · يعقوب ولد يهوذا

3 واخوته · يهوذا ولد فارس وزارا مــن

ثامر · فارس ولد اسروم · اسروم ولد

4 ارام · ارام ولــد اميناذب · اميناذب

ولــد ناسون · ناسون ولــد سلــمــون

In the name of the Father, and of the Son, and of the Holy Ghost; one God. We begin in the name of our Lord Jesus the Christ to write the Gospel of Matthew, the pure Evangelist. The first Lesson from it is read on the night of the Pure, holy Birth. The book of the generation Matt. i. 1 of Jesus the Christ, son of David, son of [I]brahîm; Ibrahîm begat 2 Isaac; Isaac begat Jacob; Jacob begat Judah and his brethren. Judah 3 begat Phares and Zara of Thamar; Phares begat Esrom; Esrom begat Aram; Aram begat Aminadab; Aminadab begat Ñason; Nason begat 4 Salmon;

ومن خروج بنى اسرائيل من مصر والى دا ود النبى
عليه السلام سنمايه واربعين سنه
ومن داود النبى عليه السلام والى
الاسكندر بن فليس الىونانى سنمايه بسبعه
وتلتين سنه ومن الاسكندر بن فليس
اليونانى الى الجنسد سندما وخلعت
ليسوع المسيح لدلزه السجود ثلثمايه وحمسين سنه
وموسيدا المسيح لدلزه السجود والى هن
السنه وهو الوصل المصقول الروحانيه
وحمسه وحمسين سنه ويكون الماصى
سنى العالم والى احرهدك السنه سنه
مسدالعه سنمايه وتلده وعابن سنه
وملام و الى يسذا المسيح حمرالعه وحمرايه سنه
مسيح نطبابه

Sermons, Legends, Martyrdoms, Epistle of Abgar, etc.
Sinai Cod. Arab. 445.
f. 77 b.
A.D. 1175.

XI. SINAI COD. ARAB. 445. A.D. 1175.

Sermons, Legends, Martyrdoms, Epistle of Abgar, etc.

f. 77^b ومن خروج بنى اسرايل من مصر والى داوود النبى
علـيـه الـسـلام سـتـمـايـة واربـعـيـن سـنـة
ومـن داوود النبى عـلـيـه السلام والـى
الاسـكـنـدر بن فـلـبس اليونانى ستمايـة وسبعة
وثـلـثـيـن سنة ومن الاسـكـندر بن فيلبس
الـيـونـانـى الى تـجـسـد سـيـدنـا ومـخـلـصـنـا
يـسوع المسيـح لذكره السجود ثلثماية وخمسين سنة
ومن سيدنا المسيح لـذكـره السجود والى هذه
الـسـنـة وهـو الـعـرض المقصود الـف ومـايـة
وخمسة وخمسين سنة ويكون الماضى من
سنـى العالـم والـى اخـر هـذه السنة سنـة
سـتـة الـف سـتـمـايـة وثلثة وثمانين سـنـة
ومن ادم والى سيدنا المسيح خمس الف وخمسماية سنة
السبح لله دايما امين

And from the exodus of the children of Israel from Egypt to David the Prophet—peace be upon him—six hundred and forty years. And from David the Prophet—peace be upon him—to Alexander, son of Philip the Greek, six hundred and thirty-seven years. And from Alexander, son of Philip the Greek until the Incarnation of our Lord and Saviour Jesus the Christ—let there be adoration at the recollection of Him—three hundred and fifty years. And from our Lord the Christ—let there be adoration at the recollection of Him—to this year, which is the intended era, a thousand one hundred and fifty-five years. And what is past of the years of the world to the end of this year are six thousand six hundred and eighty-three years. And from Adam until our Lord the Christ five thousand five hundred years.

Praise be to God continually.

Gospels.
Sinai Cod. Arab. 82.
f. 3 a.
A.D. 1197.

XII. SINAI COD. ARAB. 82. A.D. 1197.

Gospels.

اول   متى

f. 3ᵃ بسم الاب والابن والروح القدس الاه واحد

نبتدى بعون الله وحسن توفيقه وارشاده وتسديده

نكتب الاربع اناجيل المقدسة ٫ الاول من ذلك بشارة

القديس متى الانجيلى ∴ اول قراة منه ليوم الاحد قبل

الميلاد الجديد للنسبة ∴

كتاب مولد يسوع المسيح ابن داوود ابن ابراهيم ·

ابراهيم ولد اسحق · اسحق ولد يعقوب · يعقوب ولد يهوذا

واخوته · يهوذا ولد فارس وزارخ من ثامر · فارص ولد

حصرون · حصرون ولد ارام · ارام ولد عنميناذاب ·

عنميناذاب ولد ناصهون · ناصهون ولد صلمون · صلمون

ولد باعاز من راحاب · باعاز ولد عوبيد من راعوث ·

عوبيد ولد يسى · يسى ولد داوود الملك · داوود الملك

ولد سليمان من امراة اوريا · سليمان ولد يوربعام

يوربعام ولد ابياذ · ابياذ ولد اسا · اسا ولد يوسافاط ·

يوسافاط ولد يورام · يورام ولد عوزيا · عوزيا ولد

يوثام · يوثام ولد اخاز · اخاز ولد حزقيا · حزقيا

ولد منسى · منسى ولد امون · امون ولد يوشيا · يوشيا

In the name of the Father and of the Son and of the Holy Ghost, one God. We begin by the help of God and the favour of His grace, and His guidance and direction to write the four Holy Gospels; the first of these is the Gospel of Saint Matthew the Evangelist. The first reading from it is for the Sunday before the new Nativity, about the Genealogy.

The Book of the Birth of Jesus the Christ, the son of David, the son of Ibrahîm. Ibrahîm begat Isaac; Isaac begat Jacob; Jacob begat Jehuda and his brethren; Jehuda begat Faris and Zarah of Thamar; Faris begat Hesron; Hesron begat Aram; Aram begat Amminadab; Amminadab begat Naason; Naason begat Salmon; Salmon begat Boaz of Rahab; Boaz begat Obed of Ruth; Obed begat Jesse; Jesse begat David the king; David the king begat Sulaiman of the wife of Uria; Sulaiman begat Jeroboam (*sic*); Jeroboam (*sic*) begat Abiud; Abiud begat Asha; Asha begat Josaphat; Josaphat begat Joram; Joram begat Uzziah; Uzziah begat Jotham; Jotham begat Ahaz; Ahaz begat Hezekia; Hezekia begat Manasse; Manasse begat Amon; Amon begat Josiah; Josiah

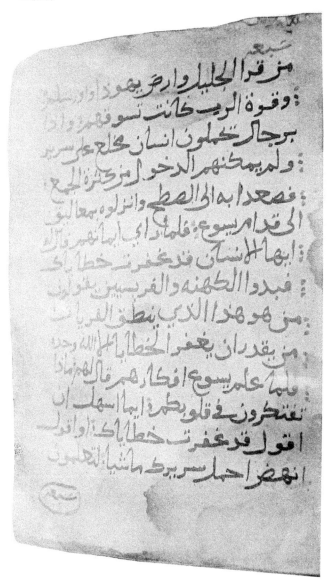

Lectionary of the Gospels.
Sinai Cod. Arab. 117.
f. 48 a.
A.D. 1204.

XIII. SINAI COD. ARAB. 117. A.D. 1204.

Lectionary of the Gospels.

سبعة

f. 48^a مـن قـرا الجليل وارض يـهـوذا واورشلم

وقـوة الـرب كـانـتَ تشفيـهـم¹ : واذا

برجال يحملون انسان مخلع على سرير

ولم يمكنهم الدخول مـن كثرة الجمـع :

فصعدا به الى الصطح وانزلوه بمعاليق

الى قدام يسوع : فلما راى ايمانهم قال له

ايهـا الانسان قـد غـفـرت خطايـاك :

فبدوا الكهـنـة والفريسيين يقولون :

مـن هـو هذا الذى ينطق الفريات :

مـن يقدر ان يغفر الخطايا الا الله وحده :

فلما علم يسوع افكارهم قال لهم : ماذا :

تفتكرون فــى قلوبكم : ايما اسهل ان

اقول قـــد غفرت خطاياك : او اقــول

انهض احــمــل سريرك ماشيا : لتعلمون

سبعة

¹ Cod. تسوقهم

from the towns of Galilee, and the land of Judea, and Jerusalem : and the power of the Lord healed them. And behold men bringing a palsied man upon a bed, and they could not enter for the multitude of the crowd ; and they went up with him to the roof, and let him down by hooks before Jesus. And when He saw their faith, He said unto him, O man, thy sins have been forgiven thee. And the priests and Pharisees began to say, Who is this that speaketh lies ? who is able to forgive sins but God alone ? And when Jesus knew their thoughts, He said unto them, What reason ye in your hearts ? Whether is it easier for Me to say, Thy sins have been forgiven thee, or for Me to say, Arise, and take up thy couch, walking ? that ye may know.

Luke 5. 17

بسم الأب والأبن والروح القدس الإله الواحد
هذا إعتذار هو يسننس الشماس السعيد خازن الكنيسة
القسطنطين المجيدة الملوكة المولود على الغد الرومزرك؟
عنهذا المصحف ※
انت يا أعز الملوك وأشرفهم لعلك استشعرت فيناهمة عظيمه
جليله ٠ فاذ عزت ان نفسي لك بلفظ يسير ذكرا يشتمل على
خبر المدريسين ٠ المعبد لهمة ء أدوار السنه الدائرة ٠ فاذ كنت
انا بعدهم ٠ ولما انهم الذي كان يجدلي فيه ان اعاينهم
بذاتي ٠ واستنفهم طمأن من ذاتي اخبارهم ٠ وما وجدت
مع ذلك مصفيان مختلفين يستخبر المستخبر منهم ٠ ويبين
الصرف من وصفهما لترليل صلاة لله ٠ اذ ثبت بذاتي ٠ واحتسبت
ايضا انه ٠ يجب علي ان اذعنلما اشارت اليه هامتك الجليله
الملكيه ٠ فرتبت من اخبارهم المكتوبه عنهن من كان كلة واحد
منهم ٠ ولا من كان ٠ وحددت الوقت الذي كان فيه ٠ وحال
جهاده وظفره ٠ وثبت ذلك للحاضرين ٠ وحملت لتصديق ما
اذكره منسوبا الى الذين كتبوا اخبارهم اولا ٠ وليركان قولي
فهذا
غير منفي خابيا من كانة تأكيد المعاني التي يخفقه ٠
هو دليل على نقض على الواصل الى الغاية القصوى ٠ واما معنى
ذلك ٠ بل دا لا تكرم كل واحدمنهم قلقعضع ء الاوصاف
التي ينبغي يلازم الضرورة السجيه الصالحه التي اعتمدوها ٠ ولقص
النصيحه التي تعرضوا عنها وتصور الكلام ء أدوا الهدى على
جمله اختصاصها ٠ مع ان هذا محتاج الى زمان طويل ٠ ولعجز ولي

Apology of Evaristus.
Sinai Cod. Arab. 420.
A.D. 1219.

XIV. SINAI COD. ARAB. 420. A.D. 1219.

Apology of Evaristus.

بسم الاب والابن والروح القدس الاه واحد
هذا اعتذار هورستس الشماس السعيد خازن الكتب ⊙
الى قسطنطين المجيد فى الملوك ⊙ المولود على القز القرمزى ⊙
عن هذا المصحف

انت يـا اعز الملوك واشرفهم لعلك استشعرت فينا همة عظيمة
جليدة ⊙ فاوعزت ان ننشى لك بلفظ يسير ذكرًا يشتمل على
خبر القديسين ⊙ المعيد لهم فى ادوار السنة الدايرة ⊙ فاذ كنت
انا بعدهم فى زمانهم الذى كان يتجه لى فيه ان اعاينهم
بذاتي ⊙ واستمعهم واظهر من ذاتى اخبارهم ⊙ وما وجدت
مع ذلك مصنفين يستخبر المستخبر مـنـهـم ⊙ ويـمـيـز
الصدق من وصفهم الجزيل ضلالة ⊙ ارتيت بذاتي فى امرك واحتسبت
ايضًا انه يجب علي ان اذعن لما اشارت اليه همتك[1] الجليلة
الملكية ⊙ فرسمت من اخبارهم المكتوبة عنهم ⊙ من كان كل واحد
منهم ⊙ وُلد من كان ⊙ وحددت الوقت الذى كان فيه ⊙ وحال
جهاده وظفره ⊙ ورتبت ذلك للحاضرين ⊙ وجعلت تصديق ما
اذكره منسوبًا الى الذين كتبوا اخبارهم اولًا ⊙ ولين كان قولي
غير منمق خاييًا من كافة تاكيد المعانى التى تحققت[2] ⊙ فهذا
هو دليل على نقص علمي الواصل الى الغاية القصوى ⊙ وانا معترف
بذلك ⊙ بل ولا تكريم كل واحد منهم قد وضع فى الاوصاف
التى تنمى بلازم الضرورة السجية الصالحة التى اعتمدوها وتقصر
النقيصة التى اعرضوا عنها وتصور الكلام فى ادوا الهوى على
جهة انخفاضها ⊙ مع ان هذا محتاج الى زمان طويل وتعب جزيل

---

¹ Cod. هامتك   ² Cod. تحققه

In the name of the Father, and the Son, and the Holy Ghost, one God. This is the Apology of Hauristus the blessed deacon, custodian of the books. To Constantine, the glorious among kings; born in the purple silk.

About this book.

Thou, O most mighty and noble of kings! that thou mightest make known among us thy great and steadfast care, didst command that we should set forth unto thee in easy language memoirs which shall contain the history of the saints, who are celebrated in the circuits of the revolving year. And behold, I am later than they in their time, wherein I might have seen them personally, and listened to them and made known their histories myself. And I did not find with this any authors from whom the seeker could enquire, and distinguish what is trustworthy in their very erroneous narrative. I have thought for myself about thy command, and have considered also that it is my duty to obey when thou hast indicated thy glorious royal care about it. And I have sketched the histories written concerning them; who each one of them was, and whose child he was. And I have defined the period in which he was, and the condition of his conflict and his victory. And I have set this in order for those who are present. And I have referred the verification of what I record to those who have first written their histories. And if my speech be without ornament and fails altogether to establish the ideas which are ascertained, this is a proof of my want of learning which reaches an extreme point, and I confess to this. But without flattery, each one of them has had attributed to him the qualities which of necessity were increased by the good disposition for which they gave him credit; the defects which he sought to avoid were minimized, and figurative speech in the infirmities of [their] desire [has been used] in the direction of moderation; though this will require a long time and great labour.

Commentary on Proverbs and the Prophets.
Sinai Cod. Arab. 13.
f. 115 a.
A.D. 1222.

XV. SINAI COD. ARAB. 13. A.D. 1222.

Commentary on Proverbs and the Prophets.

f. 115ᵃ بســمر الاب والابـــن والــروح الـــقـــدس ·

يَـوم الثـلـثا بـالـعـشى مـن الجمعة الـرابـعـة

من بعد الفصح وهو ليلة عيد نصف الخمسين

ثَـلـث قـراات الاولـة مـن سـفـر اشعيـا ·

هكذا يقول الرب مـن صهيون تـخـرج الشريعة

وَكلمة الرب من اورشليمر ويحكم بين شعوب كثيرة ·

وَيوبخ امما اعزا فى البعد لان جميع الشعوب

يَسلكوا كل واحد فى طريقه · ونحن نسلك باسم

اَلرب الاهنا الى الابد · ويملك الرب علينا من الان والى

اَلدهر · هكذا يقول الرب الضابط الكل فلتسمع

اَلتلال والاودية وكُل اساس اعوار الارض · ان

اَلرب يدين شعبه ولاسرايل يوبخ قايلا · يا شعبى ما

ذا فعلت بك ام بماذا احزنتك · اجيبنى المر اصعدك

من ارض مصر · ومن بيت نير العبودية نجيتك · ه

وارسلت قدامك موسى وهرون يـا شعبى اكثـر

[ب]ما فعلت مـعـك · هـوذا مـعـانديك انظر بماذا

جازيتـهـمر · قـد افديتك ايـهـا الاثـيـم وارشدتك

In the name of the Father, and of the Son, and of the Holy Ghost. The third day at the supper of the fourth Friday after the Passover (Easter) that is, the night of the feast of half Pentecost. Three readings, the first from the Book of Isaiah. Thus saith the Lord, From Sion the law shall go forth, and the word of the Lord from Jerusalem, and He shall judge among many peoples, and reprove mighty nations in the distance, because all peoples walk every one in his own way, but we will walk in the name of the Lord our God for ever. The Lord shall rule over us from now for ever. Thus saith the Lord Almighty, and Micah 6. 2 hear, ye hills and ye valleys, and all ye chasms, foundations of the earth. For the Lord shall judge His people, and shall rebuke Israel, 3 saying, O my people, what have I done to thee, or wherewith have I grieved thee? Answer me, did I not bring thee up out of the land of Egypt, and from the house of the yoke of bondage? and I sent Moses and Aaron before thee. O my people, I have done much for thee, behold, see how I have rewarded thine adversaries, and I have redeemed thee, the sinner, and guided thee.

ولا تسمعها بالليل سنص ومنشى بره فيمزا بالنهار
يزيل صوته ۞ وقد قال النبي الجبال الشامخه
للاراع والصخر ملجى للارانب ۞ والمناون والقمر
قصعه لاوقانه ۞ والشمس وعرفت عزوبها ۞
جعل ظلاما فصار ليلا ۞ وما هوان عظم الليل
الا وقد افتقر الانسان بالجميع واسطن
الوحوش ۞ يطلب كل واحد منها الغذا الذي
يعطيه خالقه ۞ واذا احضر النهار اجتمعت
الوحوش وقصد كل انسان عمله ۞ واذ عن
بعضا العصر يكلمه الطبيعه وناموسها ۞ واذا
ارذت الاكثر والاخص من هذه الاسيا فقلت
ان الترتيب اخط مزاجام بالطو ودور تبير
يطف فجعل الانسان حيوانا ناطقا ۞ وربط
الزعام مع العقل زباطاسن بالامدى الطاير
سرحه ۞ وربط العقل مع الروح القدس
واحيى ۞ ولكما اى بعد ۞ طر اجه
صهز طاص وانصاصاى ى واحصه

Sermons of Gregory XXI. (XXXII.)
Sinai Cod. Arab. 276.
f. 139 b.
A.D. 1225.

XVI. SINAI COD. ARAB. 276. A.D. 1225.

Sermons of Gregory. XXI. (XXXII.)

ولا شمسا بالليل تنقص وتمتلى ولا قمرا بالنهار f. 139ᵇ

يزيد ضوه ·· وقد قال النبى الجبال الشامخة

للايل ·· والصخر ملجا للارانب ·· والقنافذ والقمر

فصنعه لاوقات ·· والشمس فعرفت غروبها ··

جعل ظلاما فصار ليلا ·· وما هو ان يحضر¹ الليل

الا وقد انقبض الانسان بالهجوع وانبسطت

الوحوش ·· يطلب كل واحد منها الغدا الذى

يعطيه خالقه ·· واذا حضر النهار اجتمعت

الوحوش وقصد كل انسان عمله ·· واذعن

بعضا لبعض بكلمة الطبيعة وناموسها ·· واذا

ازدت الاكبر فالاخص من هذه الاشيا قلت

ان الترتيب احدّ مزاجا من ناطق وذوى غير

نطق ·· فجعل الانسان حيوانا ناطقا ·· وربط

اى التراب

الرغام مع العقل رباطا سريا لا يمكن الكلام

يشرحه ·· وربط العقل مع الروح القدس

والمحيى ·· ولكيما ياتى بعجيبة عظمى فى جبلته

ظهر خلاص وانتقاضا فى شى واحد ··

¹ Cod. يحظر

and no sun in the night waning and waxing; no moon in the day increasing her light. And the prophet said, the high mountains are for the goat, and the rocks are a refuge for the conies, and the hedgehogs; and the moon hath he made for the seasons, and the sun knoweth his going down. He made darkness and it became night; and no sooner does the night come on, when man contracts himself in sleep, and the wild

Ps. 104. 18

beasts wander about. Every one of them seeks the food which his Creator giveth him. And when it is day, the wild beasts assemble and every man attends to his work, and they give way to each other by the word and law of Nature. I shall add the greatest and the most special of those things; I shall say that the order has prescribed a mixture of rational and irrational. He hath made Man a rational animal; and He hath bound mould with mind by a secret bond, which speech cannot express. He hath bound mind with the Holy Spirit, the Giver of life; and in order that He might produce the greatest wonder in His creation, He caused salvation and destruction to appear in one thing.

XVII.

Lessons from the Gospels.
Sinai Cod. Arab. 122.
f. 109 a.
A.D. 1229.

XVII. SINAI COD. ARAB. 122. A.D. 1229.

Lessons from the Gospels.

f. 109ᵃ فعل اللاهوت · وكما ان الحديد اذا احمى بالنار · يفعل
فعل النار · فى الاحتراق · كذلك جسد الرب لما ايتحد
بـالكلـمة يفعل فعل اللاهوت¹ · وكان غـرض السيد
اقامـة هـذا الشاب · ولعـازر ولابنـة رييس الـجماعة
من الموت · ليحقق لنا بذلك القيامة الكلية وليحقق
بذلك ايضا قيامته التى . كانت عتيدة ان تكون بعد الـمه

يقرا فى السبت الـرابـع بعد راس
السنة من بشارة لوقا الانجيلى

فى ذلك الزمان مضى ايسوع فى السبت يمشى بين الزروع
وكانوا تلاميذه ينقوا السنبل يفركوا بايديهم وياكلوا
وان اناس من الفريسين قالوا لهم · لماذا تفعلوا ما لا يحل ان
يعمل فى السبوت · اجاب ايسوع فقال لهم · ولا هذا ما قراتم
الذى فـعـل داوود حين جاع هو والذين كانوا معه
كيف دخل الى بيت الله واكل خبز التقدمة · واعطا
للذين كانوا معه · الذى لم يكن يحل ياكله الا الكهتة وحودهم

¹ Cod. الاهوت

the action of the Godhead. As also iron, when it is heated in the fire,
does the work of the fire in burning, thus the body of the Lord, when it
is joined to the Word, does the work of the Godhead. The Lord wished
the resurrection of this youth, and of Lazarus, and of the daughter of
the ruler of the synagogue from death, that He might by it assure us
of the general resurrection, and by it assure us also of His resurrection
which was about to happen after His suffering.

To be read on the fourth Sabbath after New Year's day, from the Gospel of Luke the Evangelist.

At this time Jesus went on the Sabbath to walk among the corn-fields; and His disciples plucked the ears of corn, rubbing them in their hands and eating. And certain of the Pharisees said unto them, Why do ye that which is not lawful to do on the Sabbath-days? Jesus answered and said unto them, Is not this what ye have read that David did when he was hungry, he and they who were with him, how he went into the house of God, and did eat the shew-bread, and gave to those who were with him, which it is not lawful to eat, but for the priests alone?

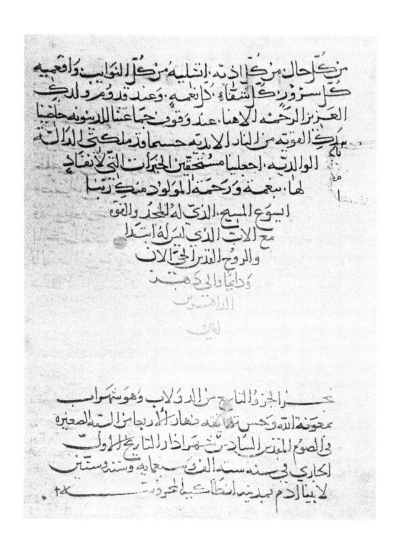

Sermons and Martyrdoms. Epistle of Abgar, etc.
Sinai Cod. Arab. 408.
A.D. 1258.

XVIII. SINAI COD. ARAB. 408. A.D. 1258.

Sermons and Martyrdoms. Epistle of Abgar, etc.

من كل حال · من كل اذية · انشليه من كل النوايب · وافعميه

كـل سرور · كـل شـفـاء كـل نـعـمـة · وعـنـد قدوم ولدك

الـعـزيـز الرحمة الاهنا · عنـد وقوف جماعتنا للدينونة خلصنا

بيدك القوية من النـار الابدية حسبما قد مـلـكتـى الدالـة

الـوالـديـة · اجعلـيـنـا مستحقيـن الخـيـرات التـى لا نـفـاد

لها · بنعمة ورحمة المولود منك ربنا

ايسوع المسيح · الذى له المجد والقوة

مع الاب الذى ليس له ابتدا

والروح القدس الحى الان

ودايما والى دهر

الداهرين

امين

نـجـز الـجـزو الـتـاسـع مـن الـدولاب وهـو شـهـر اب

بمعونة اللـه وحسن توفيقه نهار الاربعا مـن السبة الصغيرة

فـى الـصـوم الـمـقـدس الـسـادس شـهـر اذار الـتـاريـخ الاول

الـجـارى فـى سـنـة سـتـة الـف وسبعمـايـة وستة وستين

لابينا ادم بمدينة انطاكيا المحروسة +

From every condition, and from every hurt; lift him out of all misfortunes, and fill him with all joy, all healing, all grace, and at the return of thy Son, illustrious in mercy, our God, when we shall all stand for judgment, save us by thy powerful hand from everlasting fire, according as thou dost possess parental fondness. Make us meet for the good things which never pass away, by the grace and mercy of

Him who was born of thee, our Lord Jesus the Christ, to whom be glory and power with the Father who hath no beginning, and the Holy Ghost, the Living, now, and always, and to endless ages. Amen.

The ninth part of the Labyrinth is ended. The month of Ab, by the help of God and the grace of His guidance, the Wednesday of the little week, in the holy fast, the sixth month, Adâr, the first date, occurring in the year 6766 from our father Adam, in the protected[1] city of Antioch.

[1] i.e. by God.

Gospels.
Sinai Cod. Arab. 95.
f. 101 b.
A.D. 1272.

XIX. SINAI COD. ARAB. 95. A.D. 1272.

Gospels.

لا يمكن ان يخرج بشى الا بالصوم والصلاة Mark 9. 29 f. 101ᵇ
30 وخرجوا من هناك وكانوا يترددون
31 فى الجليل ∴ وما شا ان يعلم واحد لانه عرف
تلاميذه · وقال لهم ان ابن البشر
سيدفع الى يدى الناس فيقتلوه ∴ واذا ما
32 قتلوه يقوم فى اليوم الثالث فلم يفهموا
الكلمة وخشوا ان يسلوه
33 لعيد القديس اغناتيوس ثم وافوا كفر
ناحوم فلما صاروا فى المنزل قال
لهم ما الذى كنتم تفكرون فيه فيما
34 بينكم فى الطريق · فصمتوا ∴ لانهم كانوا
يتقاولون فيما بينهم فى الطريق
35 ايهم اعظم فاذ جلس دعى الاثنى
عشر وقال لهم من

cannot come out by anything, but by fasting and prayer. ³⁰And they went Mark 9. 29
out from thence, and travelled about in Galilee. And He did not wish
that any one should know, ³¹for He told His disciples. And He said
unto them that the Son of man will be delivered into the hands of
men, and they will kill him. And when they have killed him, he will
rise the third day. ³²And they understood not the words, and they feared
to ask Him.

For the feast of Saint Ignatius. ³³Then they arrived at Capernaum;
and when they were in the house, He said unto them, What were ye
considering about among yourselves in the way? ³⁴And they were silent,
for they had debated amongst themselves in the way which of them was
the greatest. ³⁵And when He had sat down, He called the Twelve, and
said unto them, He

Discourses of Mar Ephraim.
Sinai Cod. Arab. 439.
f. 216 b.
A.D. 1280.

XX. SINAI COD. ARAB. 439. A.D. 1280.

Discourse of Mar Ephraim.

f. 216ᵇ القديس مار افرام قاله على الابهات
الذين تنيحوا قلبي يوجعنى ⊙ فاتوجعوا
معـي يـا ايـهـا الاخوة وعبيد المسيح
المباركين ⊙ هلموا واسمعوا الان نفسى
حزينة وكلاي وجعة ⊙ ايـن هـى الدموع
واين هو التخشع حتى احمر جسدي بالدموع
من ينقلنى ويضعنى فى موضع لا سكن
حيث لا اسمع البتة بنى النـاس حيث
ليس بلبلة تقطع الدموع · ولا خلطة يمنع
النـوح · حيث هـو الـهـدو او السكـوت
فـارفع صوتي الى الله · واقول بالتنهد
اشفينى يا رب · فاستشفى ⊙ لان قلبي
وجع وتنهده ليس يتركنى ان اجد
راحة طرفة عـين ⊙ فانى يا سيد ارى
مـثـل الـذهب المختار كذلك تاخذ
قـديسك مـن هـذا العـالـم البطال
وكمثل ما ان الفلاح اذا ما ابصر الاثمار·
انـهـا قـد بلغت اوانـهـا وجـادت يقطفها
بسرعة لكيما لا ترزا مـن المضادين ⊙

the holy Saint Ephraim—he said it about the Fathers who have gone
to rest. "My heart pains me; and be ye pained with me, O ye brethren
and blessed servants of the Christ! Come and listen now. My soul
is grieved and my reins are pained. Where are the tears? and

where is the repentance until I bathe my body with tears? Who will transport me and put me down in a place without habitation? where I shall not hear at all the sons of men; where there is no trouble to cut off tears; nor society to prevent a lament; where there is quiet or silence. And I will lift up my voice unto God, and I will say with sighing, 'Heal me, O Lord! that I may be healed, because my heart is pained, and its sighing does not let me find rest for the twinkling of an eye. For I, O Lord! think that like proved gold, even so dost Thou take Thy saint from this vain world. And like to the husbandman when he seeth the fruit, that it is ripe, or that it is good, plucketh it hastily lest it should be hurt by the enemies;

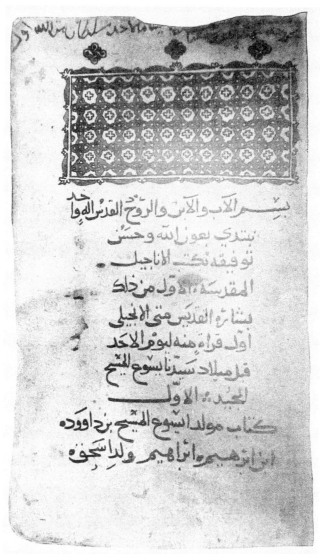

بسم الآب والابن والروح القدس اله واحد
نبتدي بعون الله وحسن
توفيقه نكتب الاناجيل
المقدسة الاول من ذلك
بشارة القديس متى الانجيلي
اول قراه منه ليوم الاحد
قبل ميلاد سيدنا يسوع المسيح
للمجيد الاول
كتاب مولد يسوع المسيح بن داوود
ابن ابراهيم وابراهيم ولد اسحق

Gospels.
Sinai Cod. Arab. 104.
f. 1 a.
A.D. 1281.

XXI. SINAI COD. ARAB. 104. A.D. 1281.

Gospels.

f. 1ᵃ بسم الاب والابن والروح القدس اله واحد

نبتدى بعون الله وحسن

توفيقه نكتب الاناجيل

المقدسة · الاول من ذلك

بشارة القديس متى الانجيلى

اول قراة منه ليوم الاحد

قبل ميلاد سيدنا يسوع المسيح

المجيد ·.· الاول

Matt. 1. 1 كتاب مولد ايسوع المسيح بن داوود·

ابن ابرهيم· ابرهيم ولد اسحق·

In the name of the Father and the Son and the Holy Ghost, one God.
We begin by the help of God and the grace of His guidance to write the
Holy Gospels. The first of them is the Gospel of Saint Matthew the
Evangelist. The first reading from it is for the First Day (Sunday) before
the Birth of our Lord Jesus the Christ, the glorious. The first Book
of the Birth of Jesus the Christ, the son of David son of Abraham.
Abraham begat Isaac.

كملت بشارة الرسول كا نجيلى الفاضل بوحنا البتول المحبوب المتكلم و اللاهيات المحمودة عز الرب وبتمامها تم نسخ الانجيل المقدس ينبوع الحياة٠٠ والمرشد الى الخلاص٠٠ ببشارة الاربعيليين المعظمين فى الرسل متى ومرقرد ولوقا ويوحنا٠ فنسال ربنا والاهنا ايسوع المسيح٠ المتجسد لخلاصنا ان يلهمنا الى عمل وصاياه٠ واوامره٠ والاستعاد عن نواهيه وزواجره٠ بشفاعة والدته العذرى البتول ورسله والبرر جاهد ولا من اجله ٠٠ ٠٠

ايها القارى اسلك بالمحبه اللاهيه صلى يا لمعفره عن الناسخ الخاطى لعلك ان برفق بالتوبه المستمى ثا هبة رأيته وكما وحدت فية الغلط والنسيان فاصلحه ان امكنك يغفر الرب لك ويستر غلطاتك امين ٠٠ ٠٠ ٠٠

كملت هذه النسخه المقدسه جعلها الله المقدير طودرسينا نار الجوه ثم رعشر من شهر ايار سنة ستة الوسيحاية وثلثة وتسعير للعام٠ وذلك ة نياسة الاب المقدير انبا ادسانيوس اسقف جبل الله٠ ادام الله دوام النير نزد بأسته٠٠ ونحنا جميعا بصلواة٠ وكان المهتم المعتنى بالورق وما يحتاج لساخته التيسر لنا الجمى المقير اخوانبا بين وهو له وللامه برهم قلاتيه ينفعه الله سافيه ولنا احمين آم

XXII. SINAI COD. ARAB. 89. A.D. 1285.

Lectionary of the Gospels.

كملت بشارة الرسول الانجيلى الـفـاضل يوحـنـا البتول المحبوب f. 164ᵃ
المتكلم فى الالاهيات¹ المحبوب من الرب وبـتـمـامـهـا تـم نسخ
الانجـيـل المـقـدس ينبوع الـحـيـاة · والـمـرشد الى الـخـلاص
ببشارة الانجيليين المـعـظـمـيـن فى الرسل متى ومرقس ولوقا ويوحنا ·
فنسال ربـنـا والاهـنـا ايسوع المـسـيـح المتجـسـد لـخـلاصـنا ان
يلـهـمـنـا الـى عـمـل وصـايـاه واوامـره · والابـتـعـاد عـن نـواهـيـه
وزواجـره · بشـفـاعـة والـدتـه الـعـذرى الـبـتـول ورسـلـه والـذيـن
جاهدوا من اجله

ايـهـا القارى · اسلك بـالـمـحـبـة الالاهـيـة² صلـى بـالـمـغـفـرة عـن
النـاسـخ الخـاطى اللابس³ ثوب الـتـوبة المسمى راهب يـراسـمـة ومـهـما
وجـدت فـيـه مـن الـغـلـط والـنـسـيـان فـاصـلـحـه ان امـكـنـك ·
يغفر الرب لك ويستر غلطاتك امين

كملت هذه النسخة المقدسة بجبل الله المقدس طور سينا نهار الجمعة
ثامن عشر من شهر ايار سنة ستالف وسبعمماية وثلثة وتسعين سنة للعالم · وذلك فى
رياسة الاب الـقـديس انبا ارسانيوس اسقف جبل الـله · ادام الـله
دوام نيرين⁴ رياسته · ورحمنا جميعا بصلواته · وكان المهتم والمعتنى
بالورق وما يحتاج لنساخته القسيس انبا اكليمى القديس اخو انبا يمين
وهو له وللامرة · برسم قلايته ينفعه الله بما فيه ولنا اجمعين امـيـن ٠:٠

¹ Cod. اللاهيات   ² Cod. اللاهية   ³ Cod. الابس   ⁴ Cod. النيرين

The Gospel is ended of the gracious Apostle the Evangelist John, the
beloved, the virgin, eloquent in Divine things, beloved of the Lord; and
its completion finishes the copy of the holy Gospel, the fountain of life,
and the guide to salvation, by the preaching of the great Evangelists
among the Apostles, Matthew, and Mark, and Luke, and John. Let us
ask our Lord and God, Jesus the Christ, incarnated for our salvation,

to inspire us to the doing of His commandments, and statutes, and the forsaking of what He has forbidden and prohibited, by the mediation of His mother, the Maiden, the Virgin, and His Apostles, and those who wrestle for His sake.

O Reader! I ask thee for the Divine Love, pray for the forgiveness of the copyist, the sinner, who is clothed with the garment of repentance, and is called the monk, Jerasimus, for whatever faults and oversights thou hast found in it; correct him if thou canst. The Lord pardon thee, and cover thy faults. Amen.

This holy copy was finished in the holy mount of God, Mount Sinai, on Friday, the 18th of the month of Ayar (May) in the year 6793 of the world, in the reign of the holy Father, Anba Arsenius, Bishop of the Mount of God. May God prolong the continuance of the lights, his rule, and have mercy upon us all by his prayers. He who took the care and trouble about the leaves, and what was necessary for the copying, was the Presbyter, Anba Clement, the holy, brother of Anba Yêmên; it is the property of him and of the Chanters for the use of his cell. May God make him profit by what is in it, and us as well. Amen.

وان يسوع قال له انطلق ايمانك خلصتك فعلى
المكان ابصر ولحق يسوع في الطريق ٩
الاصحاح الثاني والثلاثون الاخبار بامر العفو
فلما انوا الى اورشليم الى بيت فاجي وبيت
عنيا جانب جبل الزيتون ارسل اثنين من
تلاميذه وقال لهما انطلقا الى القريه الى
مقابلكما جدا على المكان عفوا امرنوطا
ما جلس عليه احد من الناس نله واذا
حلاه جيبابه الى :: فان يقل لكم احد مريضا لعلا
هذا فقولا ان الرب له به حاجه :: فيبعث بطلقه
الى هاهنا :: فمضيا ووجدا عفوا مردودا
قريا من الباب على الزقاق خارجا فحلاه
فقال لهما اناس من الوقوف هناك :: ماذا
تفعلان تحلا الجحش :: فقالا لهم كما وصاهما
يسوع فتركاهما فقادا الجحش الى يسوع ٩
والقيا عليه ثيابها جلس فوقه :: وكثيرون كانوا
يفرشون اثيابهم في الطريق واخرون كانوا
يعملانا من الشجر ويفرشون في

XXIII. SINAI COD. ARAB. 99. A.D. 1286.

Gospels.

وان يسوع قال له انطلق ايمانك خلصك ۰۰ فعلى   Mark 10. 52   f. 88ª

المـكـان ابصر ولحق يسوع فـى الطريق ⊙

11. 1 الاصحاح الثانى والثلاثون الاخبار بامـر العفو ۰۰

فلما اتوا الى اورشليم الى بيت فاجى وبيت

عنيا جانب جبل الزيتون ارسل اثنين من

تلاميذه وقال لهـما · انطلقا الى القرية التى

مقابلكما تجدا على المكان عفوا مربوطا

لـم يجلس عليه احد من الناس قط ۰۰ واذ

تحلاه جيبا به الي ۰۰ فان يقل لكم احد لـم تفعلا

هذا فقولا ان الرب له به حاجة ۰۰ فحينئذ يطلقه

الى هاهنـا ۰۰ فمضيا ووجدا عفوا مشدودا

قريبا من الباب علـى الزقاق خارجا فحلاه ۰۰

فقال لهـما اناس مـن الوقوف هناك ۰۰ مـاذا

تفعلا اذ تحلا الجحش ۰۰ فقالا لهم كما وصاهما

يسوع فتركاهما · فقادا الجحش الى يسوع ۰۰

والقيا علـيه ثيابهما فجلس فوقه ۰۰ وكثيرين

فرشوا ثيابهم فـى الطريق ۰۰ واخرون كـانوا

يقطعون اغصانا مـن الشجر ويفرشون فـى

And Jesus said unto him, Go, thy faith hath saved thee. And on the spot he saw and followed Jesus in the way.

The 32nd chapter of the narrative, Of the matter of the Colt.

And when they were come to Jerusalem, to Bethphage and Bethany beside the Mount of Olives, He sent two of His disciples, and said unto them, Go to the village which is over against you, and ye shall find in the place a colt tied, on whom never yet man sat, and when ye have loosed him, bring him to me. And if any one say unto you, Why do ye this? Say, that his Lord hath need of him, and straightway he will let him come here. And they went, and found a colt bound, near the gate, on the lane without, and they loosed him. And some of them that stood by said unto them, Why do ye do this, loosing the ass? and they said unto them as Jesus had commanded them, and they allowed them. And they led the ass to Jesus. And they threw their garments upon it, and He sat upon it. And many spread their garments in the way ; and others cut branches of the trees, and spread [them] in

هذا القول قاله و اسماى ى ماتت بيعد الله واد
قال هذا القول قال له الحقنى فالتفت بطرس
ورأى التلميذ الذي أجبه يسوع نايعا الذي
اتكا في العشا على صدره وقال يارب من هو
الذي يسلمك هذا ابصره بطرس فقال ليسوع
ياسيدى هذا ما حالة: قال له يسوع ان شيت ان
يبقا هذا الى ان اجى ماذا عليك انت الحقنى: فشاع
هذا القول فيما بين التلاميذ ان ذلك التلميذ ليس يموت
و ما قال يسوع انه ما يموت بل قال ان شيت ان يبقا
هذا الى ان اجى ما ذا عليك هذا التلميذ هو الشاهد
بهذه الاقوال و كاتبها: و قد علمنا ان شهادته صادقة
هى: و قد يوجد اشيا كثيره مما عملها يسوع لو كتبت
واحدا واحدا على حسب ظنى انه ولا العالم بعينه
كان يسع المصاحف المكتوب به حقا امين
و السبع سدا يا ابل و عليا رحمته و رافته منا بك سرمدا الز
و كان الفراع من نسخته يوم الجمعه تاسع و عشرون من
حزيران سنة ستة الاف و سبعمايه اربع و تسعين للعالم
و ذلك بدير طور سينا المقدس الرت ينفع به مقشيسهم

Gospels.
Sinai Cod. Arab. 99.
A.D. 1286

XXIV. SINAI CCD. ARAB. 99. A.D. 1286.

Gospels.

Jn 21. 19 هذا القول قاله واسما باى موت يمجد الله واذ

قال هذا القول قال له الحقنى فالتفت بطرس

وراى التلميذ الذى احبه يسوع تابعا الذى

اتكا فى العشا على صدره وقال يا رب من هو

الذى يسلمك . . هذا ابصره بطرس فقال ليسوع

يا سيدى هذا ما حاله : قال له يسوع ان شيت ان

يبقا هذا الى ان اجى ماذا عليك انت الحقنى : فشاع

هذا القول فيما بين التلاميذ ان ذلك التلميذ ليس يمُت . .

وما قال يسوع انه ما يمُت . . بل قال ان شيت ان يبقا

هذا الى ان اجى ماذا عليك فهذا التلميذ هو الشاهد

بهذه الاقوال وكاتبها . . وقد[1] علمنا ان شهادته صادقة

هى . . وقد[1] يوجد اشيا كثيرة مما عملها يسوع لو كُتبت

واحدا واحدا على حسب ظنى انه ولا العالم بعينه

كان يسع المصاحف المكتوبة حقا امين . .

والسبح لله دايما ابدا وعلينا رحمته ورافته موبدا سرمدا امين

وكان الفراغ من نسخه يوم الجمعة ثامن وعشرون من

حزيران سنة ستة الاف وسبعماية اربعة وتسعين للعالم·

وذلك بدير طور سينا المقدس ٠:٠ الرب ينفع به مقتنيه امين ٠:٠

[1] Cod. وقذ

This speech He spake, signifying by what death he should glorify God. And when He spake this speech, He said unto him, Follow Me. And Peter turned, and saw the disciple whom Jesus loved following, upon whose breast He leaned at supper, and said, O Lord who is it that shall betray Thee? Peter saw this man, and said unto Jesus, O Lord! what shall be this man's condition? Jesus said unto him, If I will that this man tarry until I come, what is that to thee? follow thou Me. And that saying went abroad among the disciples, that that disciple should not die; but Jesus said not that he should not die, but He said, If I will that he tarry till I come, what is that to thee? And it is this disciple who testifieth to these sayings, and wrote them, and we know that his testimony is true. And there are many things which Jesus did, if they were written every one, as I think, the world itself would verily not contain the books that should be written. Amen. Glory be to God continually and for ever, and on us be His mercy and pity for ever and ever, Amen. The conclusion of copying it was on Friday the 28th of Hazirân, in the year 6794 of the world, in the holy Convent of Mount Sinai. May the Lord prosper the possessors of it. Amen.

XXV.

بسم الآب والابن والروح القدس الآله الواحد
نبدي بعون المسيح وحسن
توفيقه نكتب الانجيل القدس
مرقس البشير اول قراه منه
ليوم الاحد فصل قدس الماء ه

ابتدا انجيل يسوع المسيح بن الله على ماكتب في
الانبياء هنذا ارسل ملاكي امام وجهك وهو الذي
يصلح طريقك قدامك ؛؛ صوت صارخ في البريه
اعدوا طريق الرب اجعلوا سبله مستقيمه ؛؛ كان
يوحنا يعمد في البريه وينادي بمعمودية التوبه
لاغفار الخطايا وكان يخرج اليه بلد اليهودية
كله واهل اورشليم ؛؛ ويعتمد و كلهم منه في نهر

Gospels.
Sinai Cod. Arab. 91.
f. 59 b.
A.D. 1292.

XXV. SINAI COD. ARAB. 91. A.D. 1292.

Gospels.

f. 59ᵇ بسم الاب والابن والروح القدس الاله الواحد ∴

نبتدى بمعونة المسيح وحـسـن ∴

توفيقه نكتب انجيل الـقـديـس ∴

مرقس البـشيـر · اول قراة مـنـه ∴

ليوم الاحد قبل قداس الماء ⊙ ∴

ابتدا انجيل ايسوع المسيح بن الله على ما كُتب فى

الانبيا · هنذا ارسل ملاكي امام وجهك وهو الذى

يصلح طريقك قدامك ∴ صوت صارخ فى البرية

اعدوا طريق الرب اجعلوا سبله متقومة ∴ كان

يوحنا يعمد فى البرية وينادى بمعمودية التوبة

لاغتفار الخطايا · وكان يخرج اليه بلد اليهودية

كله واهل اورشليم · ويعتمدون كلهم منه فى نهر

In the name of the Father, and the Son, and the Holy Ghost, the one God. We begin by the help of the Christ and the grace of His guidance to write the Gospel of Saint Mark the Evangelist. The first reading from it is for the Sunday before the Mass of the waters. The beginning of **Mark 1.1** the Gospel of Jesus the Christ, the Son of God, ²as it is written in the prophets. Behold, I send my messenger before thy face, and he shall prepare thy way before thee. ³The voice of one crying in the wilderness, Prepare ye the way of the Lord, make His paths straight. ⁴John was baptizing in the wilderness, and preaching the baptism of repentance for the forgiveness of sins. ⁵And there went out to him all the land of Judea, and the people of Jerusalem, and were all baptized of him in the river.

XXVI

The works of St Saba.
Bibliothèque Nationale, Paris.
Fonds Arabe 159.
f. 170 a.
A.D. 1314.

XXVI. BIBLIOTHÈQUE NATIONALE, PARIS.
FONDS ARABE 159. A.D. 1314.

The works of St Saba.

رزقنا الله بركاته . واعاننا على العمل بمفترضاته   f. 170ᵃ

واوصلنا الى ما تضمنه من عطايا الاله · ونعمة وهباته

واشركنا مع قديسيه وابراره . الذين استكملوا

حياتهم عاملين حسب مرضاته . واستحقوا ان

يتلذذوا من هاهنا بنعيمه وخيراته . له المجد والسجود

والاكرام · وعلينا رحمته . الى ابد الابدين امين .

وذلك بتاريخ الثالث عشر من كهيك[1] سنة الف وثلثين للشهدا

الابرار · الموافق للتاسع والعشرون من شهر شعبان سنة اربعة عشر

وسبع ماية للهجرة العربية . احسن الله تقضيها فى خير وعافية وامنًا

وسلامة . وناسخه الحقير المسكين بكثرة خطاياه . الغير

مستحق ان يذكر اسمه انسان من عظم خطاياه . يسال كل واقف

عليه . ان يدعوا له لكى يخلصه الرب الاله من بحار ذنوبه ويسامحه

بما فعله فى عمره من النجاسات والخطايا الكبيرة . وكلمن دعا له بشى

له امثاله . والسبح لله دايما ابدا سرمدا

---

¹ sic

This is continued on the margin of the preceding page, as follows:

وقد نقل استطرها تارخ طبخ للميرون المقدس من نسخة خط القمص نيح
الله نفسه للتذكره بدينه وكتب ذلك الحقير يحنا خادم كرسى مارى مرقس
الانجيلى بنعمة الله وكان تسطير هذا التاريخ ونقله من النسخة القديمة
فى سادس بشنس سنة ١٦١٥ للشهدا للابرار بركاتهم يـحـل علينا ويخلصنا مـن
شرايرنا الى انقضا الادهار

May God furnish us with His blessings, and assist us in doing according to His precepts; and make us attain to the divine gifts which He has pledged, and His grace and His benefits; and give us a portion with His saints and His pure ones, who have completed their lives doing according to His pleasure, and have been deemed worthy to be entertained hence by His delights and His blessings. To Him be glory and adoration and honour; and on us be His mercy for ever and ever, Amen.

And this is at the date of the thirteenth χοιάκ of the thousand and thirtieth year of the Holy Martyrs; corresponding to the twenty-ninth of the month Sha'ban the seven hundredth and fourteenth year of the Arab Hegira. May God approve its accomplishment in good and health safely and in peace. And its copyist is the mean poor man, in the abundance of his sins, a man whose name is unworthy to be called a man, from the greatness of his sins. He asks every one who comes upon this book to pray for him, that the Lord his God may save him from the oceans of his crimes, and forgive him for his wicked deeds in the course of his life; and his many sins. And whosoever shall invoke on him any blessing, unto him shall be the like thereof. And praise be to God now and for evermore.

God the Saviour.... When it was the date of the pure martyrs, the holy oil was prepared in the church of the Pure Lady Mistress Mary the Virgin in the quarter of the Greeks in Cairo the fortified, by the care of the honoured lord the Archdeacon, the wise sheikh, Wali ed Daulah, Michael the overseer of the church the above named, scribe of the Treasury and the Court, with the help of the father, the Patriarch Anba Matthew, the ninetieth in the number of the Patriarchs in the throne of St Mark. And its completion and its storing up in the holy church above mentioned was on the first day of the new week, the seventeenth of the month Pharmouthi the year of the date above.

And there were present at the aforesaid work such as were able to be present of the fathers the bishops of the North and the South: viz. Anba Isaal the bishop of the city of Anupolis, and Anba Jonas of Asioût, and Anba Isaal the Telâwy Bishop of Sidfa and the Mohalla; and Anba Moses bishop of Koos, inspired men.

And he had copied its lines, on the date of the preparation of the holy oil, from a manuscript in the hand of the *Gommos*[1], may God give rest to his soul! for a remembrance of him in his judgment. And the contemptible John, a servant of the throne of St Mark the Evangelist, wrote this by the grace of God. And the writing down of this chronicle and its copying from the ancient manuscript was on the sixth of παχών the year 1615 of the pure martyrs. May their blessing light upon us, and save us from our evil ways until the consummation of the ages!

[1] i.e. Hegoumenos.

XXVII

بسم الاب والابن والروح القدس الاله الواحد ‏السادس عشر
قصه بشارة متى السليح برجلي اخو يعقوب احد الاثنى عشر
تلاميد المسيح وهو العشار الاعلى وهو لادى واعماله فى
بلاد الكهنه وخبر شهادته شفاعته تحفظنا امين ‏؏
اما اعمال متى التى علمها فى بلاد الكهنه نوجه وهذه كما قد
نذكر وذلك ان بطرس واخاه اندراوس كانا عند
عودتهما من بلاد البرير بعد ان بيناهر فى الامانه ‏وعرفاهم
شرايع الدين وهما ساير ان فى الطريق قد لقياني هذا
وقبل كل واحد منهم صاحبه بالقبله الروحانيه ‏وقال متى
لهما اين ابتما فقال الاله من بلاد البرير دعال لهما متى وانا
ايضا قادمايت من بلاد المغوطين وانه عرف كل واحد
منهم صاحبه الاخر منا ماله من الالام ‏فقال لهما اندراوس
هذا ان المدينه التى كنت فيها قد حضر ربنا ايسوع المسيح
مع اهلها فى كل وقت وهو عندهم دايما ويعيد معهم وينصب
كرشيه فى وسط يعتهم بالغداه ويعلمهم وصاياه فلما دخلت
الى مدينتهم ونادبت فيهم وسترهم باسمه قالوا الى من يعرف
هذا الاسم فقلت لهم من عرفته ‏فقالوا الى طول رجك
وامهل علينا ولا نقل شى وتحمل هذا الغداه فانك تنظر الى الذى
بشرتنا به ‏فلما ايع من هذا حضر ربنا ايسوع المسيح وهو
راكب على جمله ... جميع قوات السما يسجونه وانا

Lives of Saints and Martyrs.
Sinai Cod. Arab. 397.
f. 27 a.
A.D. 1333.

XXVII. SINAI COD. ARAB. 397. A.D. 1333.

Lives of Saints and Martyrs.

عشر

f. 27ᵃ بسمر الاب والابـن والـروح الـقـدس الالاه الـواحـد السادس

قصه بشارة متى السليح بن حلفى اخو يعقوب احد الاثنى عشر

تلاميذ المـسيح · وهو العشار¹ الانجيلى وهو لاوى واعماله فى

بـلـدة الـكـهـنـة · وخبر شـهـادتـه شفاعته تـحفظنا امين ·

اما اعمال متى التى عملها فى بلد الكهنة فهى هذه كما قد

نـذكـر · وذلك ان بطرس واخاه اندراوس كـانا عـنـد

عودتهما من بلاد البربر بعد ان ثبتاهم فى الامانة · وعرفاهم

شرايع الدين وهما سايران فى الطريق قد لقيا متى هذا ·

وقبل كل واحد منهم صاحبه بالقبلة الروحانية · وقال متى

لهما من اين اتيتما · فقالا له من بلاد البربر· فقال لهما متى · وانا

ايضا قـد اتيت من بلاد المغبوطين وانه عرف كل واحد

منهم صاحبه الاخر مـا نـالـه من الالام· فقال لهما مثاوس

هذا· ان المدينة التى كنت فيها· قد يحضر ربنا ايسوع المسيح

مع اهلها فى كل وقت· وهو عندهم دايما· ويعيد معهم وينصب

كرسيه فى وسط بيعتهم بالغداة· ويعلمهم وصاياه. فلما دخلت

الى مدينتهم· وناديت فيهم وبشرتهم باسمه . قالوا لى نحن نعرف

هذا الاسم فقلت لهم من عرفكم به · فقالوا لى طول روحك

واتمهل علينا ولا تقلق وتعجل الى الغداة· فانك تنظر الى الذى

بشرتنا به · فلما كان من غدوة حضر ربنا ايسوع المسيح وهو

راكب على سحابة مضية· وان جميع قوات السما يسبحونه · وانى

¹ Cod. العسار

the 16th

In the name of the Father, and the Son, and the Holy Ghost, the
One God.

The history of the preaching of Matthew the Apostle, son of Halfi,
brother of James, one of the Twelve Disciples of the Christ; he was the

Publican, the Evangelist ; he was Levi ; his acts were in the town of the priests, and the narrative of his martyrdom. May his mediation preserve us, Amen.

But the acts of Matthew which he did in the town of the Priests were these, as we shall record ; and this, that Peter and Andrew his brother were on their return from the country of El Barbar, after they had established them in the faith, and taught them the precepts of religion. While they were journeying on the road, they met this Matthew. Each one of them embraced his friend with a spiritual kiss ; and Matthew said unto them, "Whence have you come?" And they said unto him, "From the country of El Barbar." And Matthew said unto them, "And I also have come from the country of the Blessed." And each one of them told his other friend what sufferings had befallen him. And this Matthew said unto them : "The city in which I have been, our Lord Jesus the Christ is present with its people at all times ; He is beside them continually, and He keepeth a feast with them. He setteth up His throne in the midst of their church in the early morning, and teacheth them His commandments. And when I entered their city, and proclaimed amongst them, and preached the Gospel to them in His name, they said unto me, "We know this Name." And I said unto them, "Who hath taught you it?" And they said to me, "Be patient, take time with us ; be not anxious nor hurried until the morning, and thou shalt look on Him whom thou hast preached unto us." And when the morning came our Lord Jesus the Christ appeared, riding upon a shining cloud, and all the powers of Heaven were praising Him. And I

بالتَّوْبَةِ ومغفرةِ الخطايا فى جميعِ الامم وَتبدون من
نَروشَليمَ واتُمْ تَشهدون على هَذا واناارْسِل اليكم
بمَوْعِد ابِى فَاجلِسُوا اشُوا فى المدينهِ يُروشَليم حتى
تَنْدَرِعُوا القوةَ من العُلّ ثُمّ اخرَجَهُم خارجًا الى
بَيْتِ عَنْيا ورَفعَ يديهِ وباركَّم وكان فِيما هُوبارِكَهُم
انفَرد عَنْهُم وصعِدالى السّمَآءِ فاتاهُم فسجَدوا
لهُ ورجِعُوا الى اورشليمَ بفرحٍ عظيمٍ وكانُوا فى
كلّ حِيـنٍ فى الهيكَلِ يُسَبِّحونَ اللهَ وُباركونَ امين

اخـراحيل لوفا بـسـلَامٍ الرّبـاِبين
فى شهرِ طُوبه سَنه خمسين والف
للشهداءِ الاطهارِ يارِّب اغفِرْ
لكاتِبه وللمُهتمِّ ولجميعِ بنى المعوديه ◉

Gospels.
British Museum OR. 1327.
f. 184 a.
A.D. 1334.

55

XXVIII. BRITISH MUSEUM OR. 1327. A.D. 1334.

Gospels.

f. 184ª بالتوبة ومغفرة الخطايا فى جميع الامم وتبدون من
يروشليمر· وانتمر تشهدون على هذا وانا ارسل اليكمر
موعد ابى فاجلسوا انتمر فى المدينة يروشليمر حتى
تتدرعوا القوة من العلا ⁖ ثمر اخرجهمر خارجا الى
بيت عنيا ورفع يديه وباركهمر وكان فيما هو باركهمر
انفرد عنهمر وصعد الى السما· فاما همر فسجدوا
له ورجعوا الى اورشليمر بفرح عظيمر وكانوا فى
كل حين فى الهيكل يسبحون الله ويباركون امين ⊙

نجز انجيل لوقا بسلامر الرب امين
فى شهر طوبه سنة خمسين والف
للشهـدا الاطهـار· يـا رب اغفـر
لكاتبه وللمهتمر ولجميع بنى المعمودية ⊙

in repentance and forgiveness of sins amongst all nations, and begin at Jerusalem. Ye shall testify about this; and I will send you the promise of my Father; and tarry ye in the city Jerusalem, until ye be armed with power from on high. Then He took them out to Bethany, and raised His hands and blessed them, and whilst He blessed them, He was separated from them, and ascended to Heaven. But they worshipped Him, and returned to Jerusalem with great joy, and were continually in the Temple, praising and blessing God, Amen.

The Gospel of Luke is completed, in the peace of the Lord, Amen.

In the month of Tûbat, the year 1050 of the pure Martyrs. O Lord! forgive its writer and the superintendent and all baptized persons.

Lectionary of the Gospels.
Sinai Cod. Arab. 628.
f. 3 b.
A.D. 1337.

XXIX. SINAI COD. ARAB. 628. A.D. 1337.

Lectionary of the Gospels.

f. 3^b بسم الاله الواحد الاب والابن والروح القدس

المقالة الاولى للقـديس متى الرسول الفصل

كتاب الاول منه ليوم الاحد قبل الميلاد المجيد

ميلاد ايسوع المسيح ابن داوود ابن ابرهيم ۞ فابرهيم ولد اسحق ۞ واسحق ولد يعقوب ۞

ويعقوب ولد يهودا واخوته ۞ يهوذا ولد فارص وزارخ من ثامار · فارص

ولد حصرون · حصرون ولد ارام · ارام ولد عميناداب · عميناذاب ولد

ناصون · نصون ولد سلمون · سلمون ولد باعاز · من راحاب · باعاز ولد عوبيد

من راغوث · عوبيد ولد ايسى · ايسى ولد داوود الملك · داوود ولد سليمن ·

من امراة اوزيا · سليمن ولد رحبيعام · رحبيعام ولد ابيا · ابيا ولد اصاف ·

اصاف ولد يوشافاط · يوشافاط ولد يورام · يورام ولد عوزيا · عوزيا

ولد يواثام · يواثام ولد اخاز · اخاز ولد حزقيا · حزقيا ولد منسى · منسى

ولد عاموص · عاموص ولد يوشيا · يوشيا ولد يوخانيا واخوته فى سبى

بابل ومن بعد سبى بابل يوخانيا ولد شلتاييل · شلتاييل ولد زوربابيل ·

زوربابيل ولد ابيوذ · ابيوذ ولد الياقيم · الياقيم ولد عازور · عازور ولد

صادوق · صادوق ولد اخين · اخين ولد اليود · اليود ولد اليعازر · اليعازر

ولد متثان · متثان ولد يعقوب · يـعـقـوب ولد يـوسف خـطـيـب مـريـم

المولود منها يسوع · الذى يدعى المسيح ۞ فكل الاجيال من ابرهيم الى

داوود اربعة عشر جيلا · ومن داوود الى سبى بابل اربعة عشر جيلا

ومن سبى بابل الى الـمـسـيـح اربـعـة عـشـر جـيـلا ۞ الـفـصـل الشانى

قراة يوم الميلاد سحر ومولد ايسوع الـمـسـيـح هكـذا كـان لـما خـطبت

مريم امه ليوسف · قبل ان يـعـتـرفـا وجـدت حبلى من روح القـدس ۞

In the name of the one God, the Father, the Son, and the Holy Ghost. The first Word of Saint Matthew the Apostle, the first chapter of it, for the first day after the glorious Birth. The Book of the Birth of Jesus the Christ, son of David, son of Ibrahîm. Ibrahîm begat Isaac, and Isaac begat Jacob, and Jacob begat Juda and his brethren. Juda begat Phares and Zarah of Thamar. Phares begat Hesron. Hesron begat Aram. Aram begat Aminadab. Aminadab begat Nason. Nason begat Salmon. Salmon begat Boaz of Rahab. Boaz begat Obed of Ruth. Obed begat Jesse. Jesse begat David the King. David begat Suleiman of the wife of Uriah. Suleiman begat Rehoboam. Rehoboam begat Abia. Abia begat Asaph. Asaph begat Josaphat. Josaphat begat Joram. Joram begat Ozia. Ozia begat Jotham. Jotham begat Ahaz. Ahaz begat Hezekia. Hezekia begat Manasse. Manasse begat Amos. Amos begat Josia. Josia begat Jechonia and his brethren in the captivity of Babel. And after the captivity of Babel Jechonia begat Salathiel. Salathiel begat Zorobabel. Zorobabel begat Abiud. Abiud begat Eliakim. Eliakim begat Azor. Azor begat Sadoc. Sadoc begat Achîn. Achîn begat Eliud. Eliud begat Eleazar. Eleazar begat Matthan. Matthan begat Jacob. Jacob begat Joseph the betrothed of Mary, from whom was born Jesus who is called the Messiah. And all the generations from Abraham to David are fourteen generations; and from David to the Captivity of Babel fourteen generations; and from the Captivity of Babel to the Christ fourteen generations. The second Chapter. Morning reading for the day of the Birth. And the birth of Jesus the Christ was thus: When Mary His mother was betrothed to Joseph, before they knew one another, she was found with child of the Holy Ghost.

XXX

الارض وامضى الارض ميلادك واكون معك الفسر أوضح
الكتاب ان لابان كان قد طلب يعقوب ومنعه حقه والجح قلب
يعقوب جلّ ولمّا نظر الله عطف وجمع قلب قوت فطنه لذلك
النذير الذي لم يعلمه لابان وللمرة وجمع قلبه وجربه
عزاه في المنام واعلمه ان الغنم سلامك وامراذلك وازّ ذلك
من يعلو واني انا الذي وطنت لهذا النذير وقوله ان ملاك
الله كلّمني وقال انا الله الذي كلّمك بيت الله يعني بيت
ابي الذي هو الاه الجوّ وانا الاجوّ مولود منه ولاذّ ذلك
البيت الذي ظهر له منه على السلم كان زسر الجماعة المستمعة
كما قد ذكر اذلك في موضعه ذلك لذكر المستجمعة وقال اجب
مستحب نصبه هنال وامره ان يعود الى ارضه الذي بها
وعله وقال اني احضرتك لهذه الارض لكي انا احد منها عني
ونعود الى ارضك وعنان معك وهكذا يريد الله متا في هذا
العالم ان يأخذ لنا منه عنا بالاعمال الصالحة وحينئذ يضع
الى ارضنا الحقيقية السماوية وخزلعنا نا جاملين
الكتاب أجابا اليا وراحيل وقالا له لعسى قد بقا
لنا نصيب اخر وميراث اخر في بيت ابينا المحسبناه عنه

Commentary of Ephraem on Genesis.
British Museum OR. 1330.
f. 198 a.
A.D. 1386 = Anno Martyrum 1102.

XXX. BRITISH MUSEUM OR. 1330. A.D. 1386.

Commentary of Ephraem on Genesis.

الارض وامض الى ارض ميلادك واكون معك التقسير اوضح f. 198ª
الكتاب ان لابان كان قد ظلم يعقوب ومنعه حقه واتتجع قلب
يعقوب جدا · ولما نظر الله عظم وجع قلب يعقوب فطنه لذلك
التدبير الذى لم يفهمه لابان ولكثرة وجع قلبه وحزنه
عزّاه فى المنام · واعلمه ان الغنم سيلدوا كمرادك¹ وان ذلك
من فعلي وانى انا الذى فطنتك لهذا التدبير · وقوله ان ملاك
الله كلمنى · وقال لى انا الله الذى كلمتك فى بيت الله يعنى فى بيت
ابي الذى هو الاله الحق وانا الاله حق مولود منه · ولان ذلك
البيت الذى ظهر له فيه على السلم كان سر للجماعة المسيحية
كما قد ذكرنا ذلك فى موضعه · فلذلك ذكر المسحة وقال حيث
مسحت لى نصبة هناك · وامره ان يعود الى ارضه الذى بها
وعده · وقال انى احضرتك الى هذه الارض لكى تاخذ منها غنى
وتعود الى ارضك وغناك معك · وهكذا يريد الله منا فى هذا
العالم ان ناخذ لنا منه غنا بالاعمال الصالحة · وحينيذ نمضى
الى ارضنا الحقيقية السماءية · ونحن لغنانا حاملين
الكتاب اجابا اليا وراحيل وقالا له لعسى قد بقا
لنا نصيب اخر وميراث اخر فى بيت ابينا · الم يحسبنا عنده

¹ Cod. كمرادك

the earth, and go to the land of thy birth, and I will be with thee"
[Commentary]. The Book explains how Laban tyrannized over Jacob,
and refused him his right, and the heart of Jacob suffered much pain.
When God saw the great pain of Jacob's heart, He made him comprehend this arrangement which Laban had not understood, and in the
greatness of the pain of his heart and his sorrow He comforted him in

a dream ; and taught him that the sheep would bring forth according to thy desire ; and this will be My doing, and I am He who hath taught thee this arrangement. And his saying is "that the Angel of God spoke to me, and said to me, I am God [*On the margin.* who appeared to thee at Bethel, and he made it certain that He who spake to him is the Son, and therefore he called Him an Angel, and God, as He in the latter time appeared. He is a Man, and God ; and therefore 'I am God,'] Who spake to thee at Bethel," which means in the house of my Father, who is very God, and I am very God, begotten of Him. And because this house in which He had appeared unto him upon the ladder, was a symbol of the Christian congregation, as we have recorded it in its place, therefore He remembered the anointing and He said : "There where thou didst anoint a pillar to Me"; and commanded him to return to his land, which He had promised him. And He said, I have brought thee to this land, that thou mayest take from it riches, and return to thy land, and thy riches with thee. And thus God wishes from us in the world that we should take from Him riches to ourselves in good works, and then we should go to our true heavenly land ; we carrying our riches. [Text.] Leah and Rachel answered and said unto him, Peradventure there remaineth to us another portion and another inheritance in the house of our father. Did he not consider us with him......

XXXI

ثم قال ان امراة ، وبعد وفانها صار اسقفا ، واعطاه الله لحمل
للاسقفية نعمة بلغ منها الى ان صارت لعجائب تكتبة له
بسّمائها ، وذلك انه اجترح عجائب كثيرة تربو على السبع ، وتجاوز
الوصف ، وما ذكر من كثرتها واحدا او اثنين ، وهي ان كان
خدام الكنيسة اودّوا في وقتٍ من الاوقات من قاد بها قليلا
فصعد ذلك على الباب ، واحتجب في ذلك اذ ما فحضرة الكنيسة
قوم يصلّون ، ولهذا السبب لم يخلج منها صوّ اكثر ، وظهرت
ملائكة سمعوا هامعه ينزل ومعز روّح ، فاما الشفاقة وحتوّه
فبيّن تياهيه منهما ما عوّض للدين واموال السنة وارعيته عنه
وذلك انه ما ازال عامص للعامّ الذي ينتظم من منهم فمنعهم من النظر
فقط ، واعطاهم كتبنا واحدا ، وصرّوه فالا لم يخدا وهذا اخني
لاسكونوا وتر سهر تر باطلا ، وسائر الرعيّة التي وتي عليها كا
يبقي ، وانقل الى طبقة الملائكة وسيرة تنظر .

بسم الاب والابن والروح القدس الاله الواحد
وصف سيرة ونيرا سيا القدس اسبين بدون صانع العجائب
اسقف مدينه ارميته وبطوّن ، لعنها او ودّ ورّس
استف بامنوا . قال يوحنا الابجيلي الذي كان الكلمه وكلمة كا
كان عند الله ، كلمه كان وحلو منه لم يكن شيء ممّا ان اباه
لنؤ اليه استعلان تعمه يا اما المستكين الذي ان بدا تر بعد تا

Legends and Martyrdoms. Labyrinth IV.
Sinai Cod. Arab. 398.
f. 129 b.
Seen December A.D. 1408.

XXXI. SINAI COD. ARAB. 398. SEEN DECEMBER, A.D. 1408.

Legends and Martyrdoms. Labyrinth IV.

f. 129^b ثم قارن امراة · وبعد وفاتها صار اسقفا · واعطاه الله لعمل

الاشفية نعمة بلغ فيها الى ان صارت العجايب تكنية له

يسمى بها · وذلك انه اجترح عجايب كثيرة تزيد على السمع · وتتجاوز

الوصف · وساذكر من كثرتها واحدة او اثنتين · وهى ان كان

خدام الكنيسة اوقدوا فى وقت من الاوقات من قناديلها قليلا

فصُعب ذلك على البار · واحتجوا فى ذلك ان ما قد حضر فى الكنيسة

قوم يصلون · ولهذا السبب لن يحتاج فيها ضوا كثيرا · فظهرت

ملايكة سمعوها معه تقول ومع روحك · فاما اشفاقه وحنوه

فيبيين تناهيه فيهما ما غرض للذين راموا ان يسترقوا رعية غنمه

وذلك انه ما ازال عارض العماء الذى اشتملهم · فمنعهم من النظر

فقط : بل واعطاهم كيسا¹ واحدا · وصرفهم قايلا لهم خذوا هذا حتى

لا تكونوا قد سهرتم باطلا · وساس الرعية التى اوتمن عليها كما

ينبغى وانتقل الى طبقة الملايكة وسيرتهم :.

بـــــــــم آلاب والابـن والروح القدس الالاه الواحد

وصف سيرة وتدبير ابينا القديس اسبيريدون صانع العجايب

اسقف مديـنة ابـريميثـونطون · الـفـهـا ثاوودورس

اسقف بافوا · قال يوحنا الانجيلى فى البدى كان الكلمة والكلمة

كان عند الله · كل به كان وخلوا منه لم يكن شى مما كان اياه

اسل واليه ابتهل ان يهب انا لى انا المسكين الذى قد بدات بهدا

¹ Cod. كيشا

Then he espoused a wife, and after her death he became a Bishop, and God gave him grace for the work of healing; he succeeded in it so that miracles became a nickname for him, and he was called after them. This was because he managed to perform many miracles, which increase with fame, and surpass narration; I will mention one or two out of the multitude of them. One was that the servants of the church were once upon a time burning few of its candles, and this was hard for the pious man. They excused themselves for this [by saying] that there were no people present in the church praying, and for this reason that much light was not required in it. Angels appeared whom they heard saying with him, "and with thy spirit." But the length to which he went in his mercies and tenderness as shown in opposing those who aimed at robbing the flock of his sheep, and this because he never ceased withstanding the blindness which overwhelmed them and prevented them from even seeing, but he gave them one purse, and he dismissed them, saying to them, "Take this that your vigil may not be in vain." And he ruled the flock with which he was entrusted as was necessary, and he was translated to the rank of the Angels, and to their life.

In the name of the Father and of the Son and of the Holy Ghost, the one God. A narrative of the life and conduct of our holy father Spiridion, worker of miracles, bishop of the city of Abrimithounton, which Theodorus bishop of Paphos(?) composed. John the Evangelist said, In the beginning was the Word; and the Word was with God, and God was the Word. This one in the beginning was with God. Everything was by Him, and without Him was nothing of what was. I ask Him and call upon Him to give me, the poor one, who has just begun upon this

XXXII.

وعظم شان هرقانوس وقوي سلطانه واستقام ملكه
واطمانت اليهود في ايامه وامنوا في جميع مساكنهم
ذكر فرق اليهود ذلك الزمان والسبب فيما جرى في انتقال
هرقانوس من الفرقه التي كان هو واباىه منها الى غيرها
وما جرى بين اليهود من العداوة والحروب والقتل بسبب ذلك
قال صاحب الكتاب كان اليهود في ذلك الزمان ثلثه فرق فواحده
يسمون الفروشيم وتفسير هذا الاسم المعتزله والفرقه الثانيه
الصدوقيه وهم من اصحاب رجل من العلما يقال له صادوق
والفرقه الثالثه يسمون الحسديم وتفسير هذا الاسم الصالحين
وهم المشتغلين بالتسبيح والعباده وكانت الصدوقيه تعادي
المعتزله عداوه شديده وتباينهم وكان هرقانوس واباوه من
المعتزله وعاداهم وكان السبب في ذلك انه صنع صنيع عظيم
واحضر فيه جميع قواده وجنوده واصحابه واحضر حكما اليهود
وهم المعتزله وحضر هرقانوس معهم فاكل وشرب فلما اخذ
الشراب منه قال للمعتزله انتم تعلمون اني واحد من تلاميذكم
واني راجع الى قولكم والمدبر برايكم ولا اخالفكم وانا
اسالكم متى علمتم بغلط قد جرى مني وخطا تعلموني به وترشدوني الى
الصواب

History of Joseph ben Gorion.
British Museum OR. 1336.
f. 43 b.
A.D. 1493.

XXXII. BRITISH MUSEUM OR. 1336. A.D. 1493.

History of Joseph Ben Gorion.

f. 43^b وعظم شان هرقانوس وقوى سلطانه واستقام ملكه

واطمان¹ اليهود فى ايامه وامنوا فى جميع مساكنهم ⊙

ذكر فرق اليهود ذلك الزمان السبب فيما جرى فى انتقال

هرقانوس من الفرقة التى كان هو وابايه منها الى غيرها ⊙

وما جرى بين اليهود من العداوة والحروب والقتل بسبب ذلك ⊙

قال صاحب الكتاب كان اليهود فى ذلك الزمان ثلثة فرق ⊙ الواحدة

يسمون الفروسم ⊙ وتفسير هذا الاسم المعتزلة ⊙ والفرقة الثانية

الصدوقية ⊙ وهم من اصحاب رجل من العلما يقال له صادوق

والفرقة الثالثة يسمون الحسديم ⊙ وتفسير هذا الاسم الصالحين .

وهم المشتغليين بالتسبيح والعبادة وكانت الصدوقية تعادى

المعتزلة عداوة شديدة وتباينهم ⊙ وكان هرقانوس واباوه من

المعتزلة وعاداهم ⊙ وكان السبب فى ذلك انه صنع صنيع عظيم

واحضر فيه جميع قواده وجنوده واصحابه ⊙ واحضر حكما اليهود

وهما المعتزلة ⊙ وحضر هرقانوس معهم فاكل وشرب فلما اخذ

الشراب منه قال للمعتزلة انتم تعلمون انى واحد من تلاميذكم ⊙

وانى راجع الى قولكم واتدبر برايكم ولا اخالفكم وانا

اسالكم متى علمتم بغلط قد جرى منى او خطا تعلموني به وترشدونى الى

الصواب

¹ Cod. واطمانت

And the dignity and power of Hyrcanus increased, and his rule was established ; and the Jews enjoyed security in his days ; and were safe in all their dwellings.

A memorial of the sects of the Jews at that period, the cause of what happened at the change of Hyrcanus from the sect to which he and his parents belonged, to another one.

And what happened among the Jews of emnity, and wars, and slaughter because of that.

The author of the book says, 'The Jews were at that time [in] three sects. The first was called the Pharisees. And the interpretation of this name is the Separated people.

And the second sect is the Sadducees. And they were the followers of one of the learned men named Zadok.

And the third sect was called the Chasidim. And the interpretation of that name is the Righteous people. And they are occupied with praise and worship.

And the Sadducees hated the Pharisees with a fierce hatred, and separated from them. And Hyrcanus and his parents belonged to the Separatists; then after that he changed to the Sadducees, and withdrew from the Separatists, and he became their enemy. And the reason of it was this; that he had made a great banquet, and had brought into it all his captains, and his troops, and his friends. And he brought thither the wise men of the Jews; and these two were Separatists and Hyrcanus was present with them; and he ate and drank. And when they took the wine from him, he said to the Separatists, "Ye know that I am one of your disciples. And I am returning to your doctrines; and I will be guided by your opinions; and I will not oppose you. And I ask you, when you have known a mistake made by me, or a fault, tell me of it, and guide me to what is right."'

XXXIII

Lectionary of the Gospels.
Sinai Cod. Arab. 121.
A.D. 1536.

XXXIII. SINAI COD. ARAB. 121. A.D. 1536.

Lectionary of the Gospels.

طالع فى هذا¹ الكتاب المبارك العبد الخاطى المسكين الكثير
السيات القليل الحسنات الطالب من السيد المسيح غفران
خطاياه وارشاده الى طريق الصواب اخطا الناس فى
الخليقة واثمهم بالحقيقة الذى لم يستحق ان يذكر اسمه فى هذا¹
الكتاب المقدس من كثرة خطاياه يواكيم باسم خورى العربى
بن المرحوم يعقوب بن المرحوم اسحاق الخياط الشوبكى
خال صقر بن المرحوم سلمان الضانى وكاتبه الخورى العربى
وهو يوم تاريخه فى الدير المقدس طور سينا الله يبيته فيه
الى يوم وفاته ويجعل له فى الكهنة حظا² ونصيب امين
وهو يسال كلمن قرا فى هذه الاسطر³ الحقيرة ان يطلب
له من السيد ايسوع المسيح الغفران يكون له نظير
ذلك من الواعد الصادق فى يوم الدين والوقوف
عن ذات اليمين بشفاعة ستنا السيدة العذرى
الطاهرة البتول الزكية ومارى موسى كليم القدرة
الازلية الالهية والقديسة العظيمة الست كاترينا
الشهيدة وجميع القديسين امين وذلك بتاريخ نهار
الثلثا المبارك عشرين يوم مضت من شهر تموز المبارك
يوم عيد مارى ايلياس النبى الحى الغيور
سنة سبع الاف واربعة واربعين لابينا ادم عليه
السلام والسبح لله دايما ابدا وعلينا رحمته الى الابد امين

¹ Cod. هذه   ² Cod. حضا   ³ Cod. الاصطر

the servant, the poor sinner, with many vices and few virtues, has studied
in this blessed book, he who seeks from the Lord the Christ pardon for
his sins, and His guidance to the right way, the most sinful of people

in the universe, and most guilty of them in truth, and who does not deserve that his name should be mentioned in this holy book on account of the multitude of his sins ; Joachim named the Arab priest, son of the late Jacob, son of the late Isaac the tailor, the Shoubky, uncle of Saqar son of the late Salmon the sheep-master. And the Arab priest wrote it ; and the day of its dating was in the holy monastery of Mount Sinai, may God make him dwell in it till the day of his death and give him a lot and a portion among the priests, Amen. He asks every one who reads these poor lines to seek pardon for him from the Lord Jesus the Christ ; that he may have [something] like this from the faithful Promiser in the day of judgment, and a place among those on the right hand, by the intercession of our mistress the Lady, the pure Virgin, the chaste maiden ; and our Lord Moses, him who held converse with the Eternal Divine Power ; and the holy great lady Catherine the Martyr, and all the Saints, Amen. And this at the date of the blessed Tuesday, twenty days having passed of the blessed month Tammuz, the day of the feast of Saint Elias, the living and zealous Prophet ; the year 7044 from our father Adam, on whom be peace, and praise be to God continually for ever ; and on us be His mercy for ever, Amen.

XXXIV

Lectionary of the Gospels.
Sinai Cod. Arab. 135.
f. 86 b.
A.D. 1558.

XXXIV. SINAI COD. ARAB. 135. A.D. 1558.

Lectionary of the Gospels.

يهلكها · ومن يهلك نفسه من اجلى هذا يخلصها · ²⁵ماذا f. 86^b Luke 9. 24

ينفع الانسان ان ربح العالم كله ويخسر نفسه ويهلكها ⊙

²⁶ومن يستحى بى وبكلماتي ⊙ يستحى به ابن البشر اذا جا فى

مجده ومجد الاب مع ملايكته القديسين · ²⁷الحق اقول

لكم · ان هاهنا اناس من القيام لا يذوقون الموت حتى

يرون ملكوت الله ⊙ انجيل ليوم الاربعا من الجمعة الخامسة

بعد عيد الصليب من بشارة لوقا الانجيلى

قال الرب لتلاميذه ⁴⁴اجعلوا فى اذانكم هذا الكلام · لان Luke 9. 44

ابن البشر عتيد ان يسلم فى ايدى الناس ⊙ ⁴⁵وانهم لم يفهموا

هذه الكلمة ⊙ وكانت مكتومة عنهم ⊙ ليلا يفطنوا لها ⊙

وكانوا يهابوا ان يسالوه عنها ⊙ ⁴⁶ثم تداخلهم فكر من

لعله ان يكون اعظمهم ⊙ ⁴⁷فعلم يسوع روية قلوبهم ⊙

فاخذ صبيًا واوقفه عنده ⁴⁸وقال لهم ⊙ من يقبل هذا الصبى

باسمي فاياى يقبل ⊙ ومن يقبلنى يقبل الذى ارسلنى ⊙ لان

من كان فى جماعتكم صغيرا ⊙ فهو يكون كبيرا ⊙

⁴⁹فاجاب يوحنا وقال ⊙ يا معلم انا راينا انسان يخرج

الشياطين باسمك فمنعناه ⊙ لانه لم يتبع لنا ⊙ ⁵⁰فقال

يسوع لا تمنعوه ⊙ فان من لم يكن عليكم فهو

معكم ⊙ انجيل ليوم الخميس من الجمعة الخامسة

بعد عيد الصليب من بشارة لوقا الانجيلى

⁴⁹فى ذلك الزمان تقدم الى يشوع احد تلاميذه وقال له ⊙ يا

معلم انا راينا انسانًا يخرج الشياطين باسمك فمنعناه

لانه لم يتبعنا ⊙ ⁵⁰وقال لهم يسوع ⊙ لا تمنعوه ⊙ فان من

لم يكن عليكم فهو معكم ⊙ ⁵¹فلما تمت ايام صعوده ⊙ اصمد

Luke 9. 24 ...shall lose it; but whosoever will lose his life for my sake, the same shall save it. ²⁵ For what is a man advantaged, if he gain the whole world and lose his soul? and make it perish? ²⁶ For whosoever shall be ashamed of me and of my words, of him shall the Son of man be ashamed, when He shall come in His glory, and the glory of the Father, with the holy angels. ²⁷ Verily I say unto you, there are some standing here who shall not taste of death, till they see the kingdom of God.

The Gospel for the Wednesday of the fifth week after the feast of the Cross, from the Gospel of Luke the Evangelist.

Luke 9. 43 The Lord said unto His disciples, ⁴⁴ Put this saying into your ears, for the Son of man is about to be delivered into the hands of men. ⁴⁵ And they understood not this saying, and it was hid from them, lest they should comprehend it; and they were afraid to ask Him about it. ⁴⁶ Then there came amongst them a reasoning, which of them should be greatest. ⁴⁷ And Jesus knew the pondering of their hearts, and He took a child and set him by Him. ⁴⁸ And said unto them "Whosoever shall receive this child in My name, receiveth Me; and whosoever shall receive Me, receiveth Him that sent Me; for he that is little amongst you, the same shall be great." ⁴⁹ And John answered and said, " O Master, we saw a man casting out devils in Thy name; and we forbad him because he followeth us not." ⁵⁰ And Jesus said, " Forbid him not; for he that is not against us, is with us."

Gospel for the Thursday of the fifth week after the feast of the Cross, from the Gospel of Luke the Evangelist.

Luke 9. 49 At that time one of the disciples came to Jesus and said unto Him, " O Master, we saw a man casting out devils in Thy name, and we forbad him, because he followeth us not." ⁵⁰ And Jesus said unto them, " Forbid him not, for he that is not against us, is with us." ⁵¹ And when the days of His ascension were finished He set

XXXV.

Lives of Saints.
Sinai Cod. Arab. 264.
f. 197 b.
A.D. 1574.

XXXV. SINAI COD. ARAB. 264. A.D. 1574.

Lives of Saints.

f. 197b قال المعتنى باخراج هذا الكتاب الى اللغـة الـعـربيـة
يجب ان تعلم ايها الاخ الفاضل الحبيب · والحبر الكامل اللبيب
ان واضع هذا الكتاب · وضعه فى سيق القديس الـعـظـيـم
صابا كوكب البرية · وكان وقتـيـذ السـيـق عـامـرا · وبـه
من القلالى اربعة عشر الف قلاية · على ما يذكر صاحب التاريخ ·
واثارها موجودة الى الان · وبعضها عامرة · وكانت حـيـنـيـذ
محشوة من الابهات الـرهبـان والـنـسـاك الـمـتـوحـديـن
مع ما ينضاف اليهم من السواح المقيمين فى الجبال والمغاير
ومثاقب الارض · الذين ليس لهم ما يشغلهم عـن اتـصـال
الصلوات والتضرع والقنوت · فـوضـع لـهـم هـذا الـتـرتـيـب
الملايم لهم · ولما كان المتورطين فى العالم · لهم اهتمام
بالاشغال الـدنيوية · والهموم العالمية · نظر الابا المتقدمون
والمعلمون السالفون فى بابهم نظر افضل · ليلا يثقل عليهم
كل الموضوع · ولا يجدون فسحة وامدا لذلك · ويتركون
الكل · ويصير ذلك سببا لعدم اكـتـراثـهـم بـالـروحـانـيـات ·
ويجعلوا كـل اهتمامهم بالجسدانيات · فخففوا عنهم بعض
الاشيا · ليبقى لهم وقتا للتصرف فى الاشـغـال · وتـحـصـيـل

He who has the charge of the translating of this book into the Arabic
tongue said, It is meet that thou shouldst know, O gracious and beloved
brother, perfect and intelligent priest, that the compiler of this book composed it in the holy and great cloister of Saba, the Star of the wilderness,
and the cloister was populous at the time. And in it there were 14,000
cells, according to what the narrator states. Traces of them are found till
now, some of them inhabited; and they were filled at that period by
the monkish fathers and the solitary hermits with such as joined them
of the anchorites dwelling in the mountains, and the caves and clefts of

the earth, who have nothing to occupy them but constancy in prayers and intercession and invocation. And there was appointed for them this order, suitable to them. And whereas those that are plunged into [the water of] the world are taken up with worldly business and mundane affairs, the ancient fathers and the early teachers thought exceedingly well about them, lest all that was imposed on them should be too heavy for them, and they should find neither time nor space for this; and they should leave all, and this should become the cause of their want of care about spiritual things, and they should give all their attention to bodily things, and they lightened them of some of the things, that there might remain to them time to occupy themselves with business and acquisition.

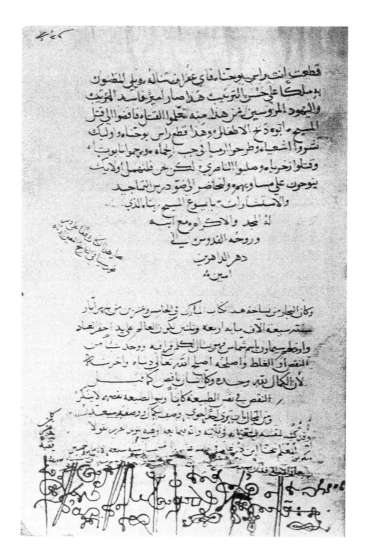

Sermons and Legends.
Sinai Cod. Arab. 423.
A.D. 1622.

XXXVI. SINAI COD. ARAB. 423. A.D. 1622.

Sermons and Legends.

قطعت انت راس يوحنا· فاى غفران تناله· ويلى المظنون
به ملكا على حسن الترتيب· هذا صار امير فاسد الترتيب
واليهود المروسين من هذا منه تعلموا القتل   فافضوا الى قتل
المسيح· ابوه ذبح الاطفال· وهذا قطع راس يوحنا· واولايك
نشروا اشعيا· وطرحوا ارميا فى جب الحماة· ورجموا نابوث
وقتلوا زخريا. وصلبوا الناصرى· لكن نحن فلنهمل اولايك
ينوحون على مساويهم· ولنحاضر الى ضو درس التماجيد
والاستشارات بايسوع المسيح ربنا الذى

له المجد والكرام· مع ابه

وروحه القدوس الى

صار هذا الكتاب وقفا على دير	دهر الداهرين
طور سينا فى التاريخ المعين ادناه	امين ∴

وكان النجاز من نساخة هذا الكتاب المبارك فى الخامس وعشرين من شهر ايار
سنة سبعة الاف ماية اربعة وثلثين لكون العالم على يد احقر العباد
وارذلهم سيماون باسم شماس فهو يسال لكلمن قرا فيه ووجد شيا من
النقص او الغلط واصلحه اصلح الله تعالى دنياه واخرته
لان الكمال لله وحده وكل انسان ناقص كما قيل
النقص فى نفس الطبيعة كاينا   وبنو الطبيعة نقصهم لا ينكر
ومن المحال بان ترى احدا حوى   وصف الكمال ووصفه متعذر
وقد كتبه لنفسه ليتعنا به فى قلايته وانه فيما بعد اوهبه للولد العزيز نقولا
[ابن] المعلم يحنا ابن درغام فى خامس عشرين ... سنة سبعة الاف وماية وخمسين

Thou hast cut off the head of John; and what pardon canst thou
obtain? Woe to me, the supposed king by a good succession. This one
became a prince who spoilt the succession; and the subject Jews have

learned murder from this one; and they got so far as to kill the Messiah. His father slaughtered the infants; and this one cut off the head of John; and those people sawed Isaiah in sunder, and threw Jeremiah into a miry pit; and they stoned Naboth and killed Zacharia, and crucified the Nazarene. But let us leave these people to sigh for their sins, that we may occupy ourselves with the light of learning praises, and asking counsel of Jesus the Messiah our Lord, to whom be glory and honour, with His Father and His Holy Spirit, to everlasting ages, Amen.

This book became the property of the Monastery of Mount Sinai at the date specified below.

The completion of the manuscript of this blessed book was on the 25th of the month of Ayâr (May) in the year 7130 of the existence of the world, by means of the most contemptible and despicable of slaves Simeon, by name a Deacon; and he asks every one who reads in it, and finds any defect or fault and puts it right, may God, the exalted, put right this his world and his other one; because perfection belongs to God alone, and every man is imperfect, as it has been said, Imperfection exists in the soul of Nature, and the defects of the sons of Nature are not unknown. And it is impossible that thou shouldst see one who contains in himself the quality of perfection, and the description thereof is impossible. And it is written for himself to occupy himself in his cell with it; and afterwards Nicola, the beloved child, son of the teacher John Ibn Darghâm, on the twenty-fifth .... in the year seven thousand and a hundred and fifty

علي صورتنا ومثال ما يعني بالاستطاعه
والسلطه والملك والتصرف بدراته
والولاوه والاختيار علي سبيل المثال
والتشرف ويحسب ما يقوى الانسان من
صورته التي خلقها في الحايط والظاهر
في المنزله من البشر هو بعينه بل
علي سبيل القوى منه واذا كان الانسان
يقوى من الله بالصوره والمثال
والله قد خلق الانسان يشبيي
بوصيه خالقه وشريعته وناموسه
وتلك الشريعه والناموس والوصايا
فيجب ان تكون تضاهب طبيعه واضعها
ومعنى سها علي جهة التشرف ومثال
ذلك اذا كان لك ولدا او عبد اوكنت
انت في طاعتك رحيما فهل انا مرو ان
يكون

Dialogue between an Emir and a Monk.
Sinai Cod. Arab. 625.
Read in A.D. 1698.

XXXVII. SINAI COD. ARAB. 625. *Read in* A.D. 1698.

Dialogue between an Emir and a Monk.

The Monk.

على صورتنا ومثالنا يعنى بالاستطاعة

والسلطة والتملك والتصرف بذاتـه

والارادة والاختيار على سبيل المثال

والتقرب وبحسب ما يقرب الانسان من

صورته التى يخلقها فى الحايط والظاهرة

فى المنزلة فترا ليس هو بعينه بل

على سبيل القرب منه واذا كان الانسان

يقرب مـن اللـه بالصورة والمثال

واللـه قـد خـلـق الانسان يستسير

بوصيـة خـالـقـه وشريعته وناموسه

وتـلـك الشريعة والناموس والوصايا

فيجب ان تكون تناسب طبيعة واضعها

ومفترضها علـى جهة التقرب ومثال

ذلك اذا كان لك ولدا ام عبدا وكنت

انت فى طباعك رحيما فهل تامره ان

يكون

"according to our image and likeness," that is to say, in power and
authority and dominion and self-control and will and choice, by way of
likeness and approach, and just as a man is like his image which he creates
upon the wall, and which appears in the house, and thou seest not himself
but something in the way of being like him, thus man approaches God
in His image and likeness. And God created man to wish to walk in
the commandment of his Creator, and in His ordinance and law; and

this is the ordinance and the law and the commandments ; and thou must necessarily be akin to the nature of their Founder and Legislator by way of resemblance. For example, if thou hadst a son or a servant, and thou wert in thy disposition compassionate, wouldst thou command him to be

Chrysostom's Commentary on the
Epistle to the Hebrews.
Sinai Cod. Arab. 626.
f. 86
A.D. 1726.

XXXVIII. SINAI COD ARAB. 626. A.D. 1726.

Chrysostom's Commentary on the Epistle to the Hebrews.

f. 86 الجسد · لان هذا الاسم الذى هو ابنه · لان كلمة الله كان

لها هذا الاسم دايماً · اعنى الافضل الذى هو الله الكلمة

لم يزل له · وما ورثه اخيراً · ولا ايضاً صار افضل من الملايكة ·

عند ما طهرنا من جرايمنا بل لم يزل افضل وافضل من غير اضافة

الى غيره · فاذاً هذا الكلام متوجه الى الجسد · وقد اعتدنا

نحن ايضاً اذا ما كنا نتفاوض فى معنى انسان مما نصفه

بما علا وتخامل والدليل على ذلك · اننا اذا قلنا ان الانسان

ليس هو شيًا · الانسان تراب الانسان رماد · فان جــمــيـع

صفاتنا هذه مرجوعها الى الانقص · واما اذا قلنا ان الانسان

حيوان غير مايت · الانسان ناطق مجانس لـلـعـلـويـن · فان

بنية كلامنا قـد تاست على الافضل · وهـكـذا قـد جـرت

الحال فى المسيح تعالى · وذلك ان السعيد بولص تارة تكلم

عليه من الجهة العالية · وتارة من الجهة المتنازلة · ايـثـاراً

ان يدل على سياسته · ويبينها وان يفيد معرفة طـبـيـعـتـه

التى لا يشوبها زوال لا غيار ⁘ المنة لله تعالى وحده

العظة الاولى

فى الدينونة وفى مضار الـرذيـلـة ومـنـافـع الـفـضـيـلـة ⊙

وفى نار جهنم مـحرقة فقط · لا مضية · وفى الرحمة ⁘ فان قد طهرنا

السيد تعالى ايها الخلاق من ما اثمنا · فالخليق بنا ان نلزم

الطهارة

the body; because this name, which is that of His Son, this name
belonged to the Word of God always; I mean that the Highest Good,
which is God, never ceased to possess the Word, and He did not inherit it
afterwards, nor did He afterwards become better than the angels, while

He purified us from our sins; but He was always better, and was better without relation to anything else; and in that case this language refers to the body; and we are accustomed also when we converse about the meaning of Man, to qualify him by what is high or low; and the proof of this is that when we say that Man is nothing, Man is dust, Man is ashes, then the result of all these our epithets is towards diminution. But when we say that Man is an immortal animal; Man is endowed with reason, akin to the supernal beings; the edifice of our speech is founded on what is best. And thus has been the case in regard to the Christ, may He be exalted! And thus the blessed Paul sometimes speaks about Him from the supernal side, and sometimes from the humble side, preferring to indicate His economy and to explain it, and to teach the knowledge of His nature, which is not affected by any cessation or change. Grace belongs to God, may He be alone exalted!

The First Sermon.

About the Judgment, and about the harm of Vice, and about the benefits of Virtue, and about the Fire of Hell which burns only and gives forth no light; and about Mercy. And since the Lord, who is exalted, hath purified us, O Thou who dost create out of water! we are guilty, and it is meet for us to cling to purity.

بحسن جمال فضايلك هاهنا انك الى الطور المقدس
دنوت وبناظرك نحو السما حدقت وعلى ذرى الجبل
باقدامك وطيت وسعيت سعيا مجدا ونهايت
ثم ركبت على ساروبيم الفضايل وطرت وصعدت
بالجبله من حيث قرت العدد وسبقت نهدت
لنا السبيل منقدما ابانا في الهدايه والارشاد
والاحرى ان نقول انك والى الان بعد بهدي جماعنا
وتتقدم في الارشاد كاننا اذ قد حاضرت
ووصلت الى هان هذا السلم البارتفه
وابتحدت بالمحبه اتحادا اكبدا
والمحبه هو الله الذي له الحد
المابد الدهور كلها
امين

Sermons of John Klimakos, Abbot of Sinai.
Sinai Cod. Arab. 339.
f. 274 a.
A.D. 1736.

XXXIX. SINAI COD. ARAB. 339. A.D. 1736.

Sermons of John Klimakos, Abbot of Sinai.

f. 274ᵃ

بحسن جمال فضائلك هاهنا انك الى الطور المقدس

دنوت وبناظرك نحو السما حدقت وعلى ذرى الجبل

باقدامك وطيت وسعيت سعيا مجدا وتعليت

ثم ركبت على شاروبيم الفضايل وطرت وصعدت

بالجلبة من حيث قهرت العدو وسبقت فمهدت

لنا السبيل متقدما ايانا فى الهداية والارشاد

والاحرى ان نقول انك والى الان بعد تهدى جماعتنا

وتتقدم فى الارشاد كافتنا اذ قد حاضرت

ووصلت الى راس هذا السلم البار نفسه

وايتحدت بالمحبة ايتحادا اكيدا

والمحبة هى الله الذى له المجد

الى ابد الدهور كلها

امين

وقف دير طور سيا المقدس فكلمن اخرجه عن الوقفية يكون محرم من الله
تعالى ومن حقارة

۱۷۳٦
سنة
مسيحية

الاب السيد نيكيفورس ريس اساقفة طور سينا المقدس وريثو الجليل

in the beauty of the loveliness of Thy virtues here Thou didst approach
the holy hill, and with Thine eye Thou didst gaze unto the heaven, and
on the tops of the mountain Thou didst tread with Thy feet, and didst
labour strenuously, and wentest up. Then Thou didst ride upon the
Cherubim, the virtues, and didst fly and ascend with a shout from where **Ps. 18. 10**
Thou didst vanquish the Enemy and Thou didst go before and spread a
path for us, preceding us in guidance and direction, and it is better for

us to say that until now Thou dost still lead us all, and dost go before us all in guidance, since Thou hast run the race, and hast arrived at the very top of that pure ladder, and hast united Thyself in love by a sure union; and Love is God, to Whom be glory throughout all ages, Amen.

The property of the Convent of Mount Sinai the holy, and every one who takes it from its possession will be cursed by God, who is exalted, and by the contemptible father the lord Nikiforos Archbishop of the holy Mount Sinai and the glorious Raithō, in the Christian year 1736.

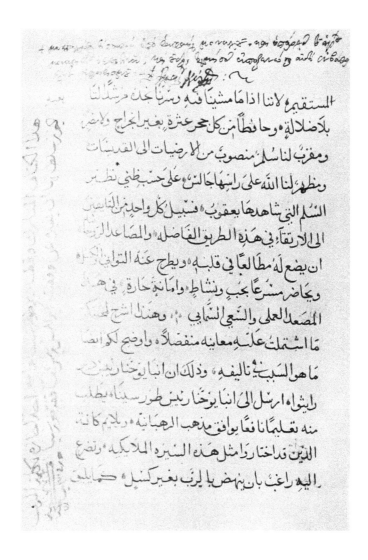

Prologue of Matthæus Raderius to the Scala Paradisi
of John Klimakos, Abbot of Sinai.
Sinai Cod. Arab. 339.
f. 3 a.
A.D. 1739.

† μετεπωλήθη τὸ παρὸν ὑπὸ ῾Ραφαὴλ μοναχοῦ, καὶ ὑπάρχει τοῦ ἁγίου μοναστηρίου ὄρους Σινᾶ, καὶ οὐδεὶς τολμήσει ἀποξενῶσαι αὐτὸ ἐν βάρει ἀλύτου ἀφωρισμοῦ. ῾Ραφαὴλ Κίνεργος.

XL. SINAI COD. ARAB. 339. A.D. 1739.

Prologue of Matthæus Raderius to the Scala Paradisi of John Klimax, Abbot of Sinai.

f. 3ª المستقيم · لاننا اذا ما مشينا فيه وسرنا نجده مرشدا لتابعيه

بلا ضلالة · وحافظا من كل حجر¹ عثرة بغير انجراح ولا مضوة

ومقرب لنا سلم منصوب من الارضيات الى القديسات

ومظهر لنا الله على راسها جالس على حسب ظنى نظير

السلم التى شاهدها يعقوب · فسبيل كل واحد من التايقين

الى الارتقا فى هذه الطريق الفاضلة والمصعاد الروحانية

ان يضع له مطالعا فى قلبه · ويطرح عنه التوانى والكسل

ويحاضر مسرعا بحب ونشاط وامانة حارة فى هذا

المصعد العملى والسعى السمايى ⁖ وهنذا اشرح لمحبتكم

ما اشتملت عليه معانيه منفضلا واوضح لكم ايضا

ما هو السبب فى تاليفه · وذلك ان انبا يوحنا رييس دير

رايثوا ارسل الى انبا يوحنا رييس طور سينا يطلب

منه تعليما نافعا يوافق مذهب الرهبانية · ويلايم كافة

الذين قد اختاروا مثل هذه السيرة الملايكية · وتضرع

اليه راغب بان ينهض بالرب بغير كسل · كما يليق

¹ Cod. جحر

the straight [way], for when we go into it, and travel, we find it guiding its followers without error, and guarding them from every stone of stumbling without wound or hurt; and bringing near to us the ladder planted from the earthly to the Holy, and shewing us God seated at its top, I suppose like the ladder which Jacob witnessed. The path of every one who desireth to climb into this excellent way, and the spiritual ascent, is to place for himself stairs of it in his heart, and throw away from himself hesitation and idleness, and present himself quickly with love and ardour and fervent faith in this practical ascent, and in the heavenly course. And thus I shall explain to you, dear friends, what its ideas contain, and shew you plainly also the reason for its composition. It is because Anba John Abbot of Raithō sent to Anba John Abbot of Mount Sinai, seeking from him useful instruction suitable to the monastic life, and meet for those who have chosen this angelic walk, and earnestly implored him to arise in the Lord, without laziness, as becometh

In a later hand.

This blessed book is the property of the Monastery of Mount Sinai; and no one has permission, by the Word of the Lord, whose authority is great, to alienate it from being its property. Cyril, Archbishop of Mount Sinai, Nisân 30, 1772, the Christian year.

XLI.

Prayers.
Sinai Cod. Arab. 587.
f. 21 b.
A.D. 1787.

XLI. SINAI COD. ARAB. 587. A.D. 1787.

Prayers.

f. 21ᵇ نمجدك شاكرين كما نمجد المسيح الاهنا القوى
العزيز الكثير الرحمة وحده · واربعين صوت
يا رب ارحم وباقى الترتيب كما مر فى الساعة الثالثة
وبعد المطانيات وتقول هذا الافشين لمار باسيليوس

اذا لم يكن مصوريون

ايها الاله رب القوات وصانع جميع المخلوقات · يا من
بكثرة تحننك ومراحمك التى لا توصف ارسلت
ابنك الوحيد ربنا يسوع المسيح · لاجل خلاص جنسنا
ولاجل صليبه الكريم مزقت منك خطايانا و
فضحت روسا وسلاطين الظلام · انت ايها السيد
المحب البشر اقبل منا نحن الخطاة الشكر والطلبات
الابتهالية وانقذنا من كل سقطات المبيد المظلم ·
ونجنا من جميع الطالبين لنا المساوى من الاعدا
المنظورين والغير منظورين · سمر من خوفك فى
لحمنا · ليلا تميل قلوبنا الى الاحاديث الباطلة · ولا

f. 22ᵃ الى الافكار الشريرة · بل بشوقك اجرح نفوسنا لكى
ننظر اليك فى كل حين · مهتدين بالنور الذى من قبلك
وملاحظين نورك الازلى الذى لا يدنى منه · وبغير
فتور · نرسل لك الشكر والاعتراف ايها الاب

الذى لا ابتدا له مع ابنك الوحيد وروحك

الكلى قدسه الصالح وصانع

الحياة الان وكل اوان والى

دهر الداهرين امين ·

تمت بعون الله

هذه الكراسة برسم الاخ كير حرکسندوس المتوحد
السينايى الله هناه بها وفتح فهمه للتعليم بما فحواها
فى ٥ اب سنة ١٧٨٧ لمحروسة طربلوس.

We grateful people praise Thee as we praise the Christ our God, the alone powerful, the glorious, the merciful. And forty times, O Lord, have mercy[1]! and the rest of the order shall be like that which passed in the third hour, and after the Matins, and thou shalt say this office to Saint Basil when there is no μεσώριον.

O God, Lord of the Powers, and Creator of all creatures! O Thou Who in the abundance of Thy love and Thy mercies, which are indescribable, didst send Thine only Son, our Lord Jesus the Christ, because of the salvation of our race, and because of His glorious cross, and hast torn up [the bond of] our sins from Thee, and hast confounded the chiefs and powers of darkness; Thou, O Thou Lord who lovest mankind, receive from us, even us sinners, thanks and imploring prayers, and save us from all errors of the Destroyer, the Tyrant; and rescue us from all who seek injuries for us, amongst the enemies, seen, and unseen. Fasten (nail) Thy fear in our flesh, that our hearts may not be inclined to vain fables, nor to wicked thoughts, but with desire for Thee wound our souls, that we may look towards Thee at all times, led by the light, which is from Thy presence, and contemplate Thy eternal light, which no one can approach.

And unweariedly we send to Thee praise and confession, O Father, who art without beginning, with Thine only Son, and Thy all-holy Spirit, the good, the Creator of life, now and at all times and to all eternity, Amen.

This book was finished by the help of God at the command of the brother Κύριος Chrysandus[1] the monk of Sinai, may God give him benefit from it, and open his intelligence for teaching about its meaning! On the 5th of Ab in the year 1787 at the fortified town of Tarablûs.

---

[1] = Κύριε ἐλείσον.

CAMBRIDGE: PRINTED BY JOHN CLAY, M.A. AT THE UNIVERSITY PRESS.